PORTFOLIO PENGUIN

HOW ADAM SMITH CAN CHANGE YOUR LIFE

'Makes you feel better about life, humanity and yourself. Like having a conversation and a scotch with Adam Smith or, even better, Russ Roberts' Nassim Nicholas Taleb, author of *The Black Swan*

'Can economists teach us how to live a good life? When the economists in question are Adam Smith and Russ Roberts, the answer is a definitive yes. Roberts shines a fresh light on Smith's ideas about morality and human nature and finds they hold up remarkably well in the twenty-first century. A fun, fascinating and original book that will challenge you to become a better version of yourself' Daniel H. Pink, author of *Drive*

'Adam Smith was not just an economist; he had penetrating insights into human nature that informed his rich, subtle and revolutionary approach to moral philosophy. Russ Roberts combines a deep understanding of what Smith was on about with a fluent writing style to bring out the surprisingly modern implications of Smith's thinking' Matt Ridley, author of *The Rational Optimist*

'Russ Roberts has taken a brilliant but difficult classic – Smith's *Theory of Moral Sentiments* – and written an engaging and inspiring meditation on virtue, friendship and happiness. The result is a wonderful guide to living a good life' Jonathan Haidt, author of *The Righteous Mind*

'Roberts whisks the reader through Smith's "hidden gem" and skillfully blends modern examples with Smith's original, leaving you wanting to tackle his masterpiece' *Financial Times*

ABOUT THE AUTHOR

Russ Roberts is the John and Jean De Nault Research Fellow at Stanford University's Hoover Institution. He hosts the award-winning weekly podcast *EconTalk* and is the author of three economics novels, including *The Price of Everything: A Parable of Possibility and Prosperity*. He is also the co-creator of the Keynes-Hayek rap videos, which have been viewed over seven million times on YouTube.

@econtalker

How Adam Smith Can Change Your Life

An Unexpected Guide to
Human Nature and Happiness

Russ Roberts

PORTFOLIO
PENGUIN

158·1

PORTFOLIO PENGUIN

UK | USA | Canada | Ireland | Australia
India | New Zealand | South Africa

Penguin Books is part of the Penguin Random House group of companies
whose addresses can be found at global.penguinrandomhouse.com.

First published in the United States of America by Portfolio/Penguin,
a member of Penguin Group (USA) LLC 2014
First published in Great Britain by Portfolio Penguin 2014
Published in this edition 2015
001

Printed in Great Britain by Clays Ltd, St Ives plc

A CIP catalogue record for this book is available from the British Library

ISBN: 978-0-241-00320-6

www.greenpenguin.co.uk

MIX
Paper from
responsible sources
FSC® C018179

Penguin Random House is committed to a
sustainable future for our business, our readers
and our planet. This book is made from Forest
Stewardship Council® certified paper.

To Sharon

CONTENTS

How Adam Smith
Can Change Your Life

Chapter 1

❧

How Adam Smith Can Change Your Life

What is the good life? Religion, philosophy, and modern self-help books grapple with the question, but the answer is elusive. Does it mean being happy? Or is it about wealth and professional success? What role does virtue play? Does the good life mean being good? Does it mean helping others and making the world a better place?

Two hundred and fifty years ago, a Scottish moral philosopher addressed these questions in a book with the unglamorous title *The Theory of Moral Sentiments*. The book was Adam Smith's attempt to explain where morality comes from and why people can act with decency and virtue even

1

when it conflicts with their own self-interest. It's a mix of psychology, philosophy, and what we now call behavioral economics, peppered with Smith's observations on friendship, the pursuit of wealth, the pursuit of happiness, and virtue. Along the way, Smith tells his readers what the good life is and how to achieve it.

The book was a success in its day. But today *The Theory of Moral Sentiments* is virtually forgotten, dwarfed by the reputation Smith achieved with his second book. That book, *An Inquiry into the Nature and Causes of the Wealth of Nations*, published in 1776, made Adam Smith forever famous and gave birth to the field of economics. While few people still read *The Wealth of Nations*, it's undeniably a famous book, a classic. Fewer still read or have even heard of Smith's other book, *The Theory of Moral Sentiments*.

For most of my career, I hadn't read it either. That's a bit awkward for an economist to confess. You'd think I would have read both major books by the founder of my field. But until recently, I knew very little about *The Theory of Moral Sentiments*. In fact, for most of my career, I never heard anyone mention Smith's other book, the not-famous one, the weird one with the daunting title that didn't sound like it had much to do with economics.

My relationship to *The Theory of Moral Sentiments*

changed when my friend Dan Klein at George Mason University suggested that I interview him about it on my weekly podcast, *EconTalk*. I agreed, thinking it would get me to finally read the book. I did at least own a copy—I had bought it maybe thirty years earlier, thinking that an economist should at least *own* both of Adam Smith's books. I took it down off my shelf, opened the book to the first page, and began reading.

> How selfish soever man may be supposed, there are evidently some principles in his nature, which interest him in the fortune of others, and render their happiness necessary to him, though he derives nothing from it except the pleasure of seeing it.

Forty-two words. A long sentence by modern standards. I had to read Smith's opening sentence twice before I understood what he was saying: that even though people can be pretty selfish, they do care about other people's happiness. Makes sense. I kept reading. I read the first page. Then the second page and the third. I closed the book. A second confession—I had no idea what Smith was talking about. The book appeared to begin in midstream. Unlike *The Wealth of Nations*, which is delightful and engaging prose from the get-go, *The Theory of Moral Sentiments* is very slow going. I had a moment of unease—maybe I shouldn't have agreed to the interview. I wasn't sure I could figure out what this book was about. I was going to embarrass myself. I thought of asking Dan to cancel.

I pressed on, hoping to find my footing. I started over. Eventually I began to get a feel for what Smith was up to. A third of the way in, I was hooked. I lugged it to my daughter's soccer games and devoured it at halftime and when my daughter wasn't playing. I started reading excerpts out loud to my wife and kids at the dinner table, hoping to get them interested in Smith's ideas about how to relate to others. The margins of the book began to fill up with stars and exclamation points marking passages I had enjoyed. By the time I finished the book, I wanted to shout from the rooftops—it's a marvel, a hidden gem, you've got to read it!

The book changed the way I looked at people, and maybe more important, it changed the way I looked at myself. Smith made me aware of how people interact with each other in ways I hadn't noticed before. He dispenses timeless advice about how to treat money, ambition, fame, and morality. He tells the reader how to find happiness, how to treat material success and failure. He also describes the path to virtue and goodness and why it's a path worth pursuing.

Smith helped me understand why Whitney Houston and Marilyn Monroe were so unhappy and why their deaths made so many people so sad. He helped me understand my affection for my iPad and my iPhone, why talking to strangers about your troubles can calm the soul, and why people can think monstrous thoughts but rarely act upon them. He helped me understand why people adore politicians and how morality is built into the fabric of the world.

And even though he's the father of capitalism and wrote the most famous and maybe the best book ever on why some nations are rich and others are poor, Adam Smith in *The Theory of Moral Sentiments* wrote as eloquently as anyone ever has on the futility of pursuing money with the hope of finding happiness. How do you reconcile that with the fact that no one did more than Adam Smith to make capitalism and self-interest respectable? That is a puzzle I try to unravel toward the end of this book.

Besides the emptiness of excessive materialism, Smith understood the potential we have for self-deception, the danger of unintended consequences, the seductive lure of fame and power, the limitations of human reason, and the unseen sources of what makes our lives both so complex and yet at times so orderly. *The Theory of Moral Sentiments* is a book of observations about what makes us tick. As a bonus, almost in passing, Smith tells us how to lead the good life in the fullest sense of that phrase.

The details of Smith's own life are fairly mundane. He was born in the village of Kircaldy, Scotland, in 1723. His father died a few months later. At the age of fourteen, Smith went off to school at the University of Glasgow, then Oxford, returning to lecture at the University of Edinburgh before being appointed at the University of Glasgow in 1751, as a professor first of logic and then of moral philosophy. His mother and unmarried aunt joined him in Glasgow at the house provided by the university. In 1763 he left academic life for a more lucrative job tutoring the wealthy young Duke of Buccleuch.

This must have been a rather dramatic change of pace for the forty-year-old Smith, giving him an intimate look at the lifestyles of the rich and famous of his day. For two and a half years, Smith traveled in France and Switzerland with the boy and, along the way, met some of the great European intellectuals of the time, including Voltaire, François Quesnay, and Anne-Robert-Jacques Turgot. After returning from Europe, he spent the next decade in Kircaldy and then London, working on *The Wealth of Nations*.

In 1778, Smith moved from London to Edinburgh to live with his mother and several cousins. That same year he was appointed one of the five commissioners of customs in Scotland, leading a bureaucracy that sought out contraband and collected duties, or what we now call tariffs. Perhaps the most influential defender of free trade in the history of political economy spent the last years of his life reducing the flow of smuggled goods and collecting taxes for the government from importers.

Other than his time in Europe, Smith appears to have led what most would call a particularly unexciting life. He was a lecturer, a professor, a tutor—three jobs that are renowned for being removed from what might be called reality. Joseph Schumpeter wrote, "No woman, excepting his mother, ever played a role in his existence: in this as in other respects the glamours and passions of life were just literature to him." Schumpeter exaggerated a bit, but Smith never married. He died in 1790 at the age of sixty-seven.

Such was Smith's outer life. What about his inner life? No journal or diary survived Smith's death—he asked that all his private papers be destroyed. With a few exceptions, most of his letters are spare and businesslike, even when he is writing his best friend, the great philosopher and his fellow countryman David Hume. How could a man of Smith's seemingly limited experience plumb the depths of human interaction and manage to dredge up any insight?

We know he managed to do so because we have *The Theory of Moral Sentiments*. First published in 1759, the book went through six editions, the last one published in 1790, the year of Smith's death, when he made substantial revisions to the text. In a sense, *The Theory of Moral Sentiments* was Smith's first and last book.

I think I know why he revised it late in his life, at a time when he was doing little serious scholarship that has survived. Once you start to think about human motivation and the bright and dark side of humanity—what Faulkner called the "human heart in conflict with itself"—it's hard to think about anything else. Trying to understand your neighbor and, in turn, yourself really doesn't get old. There's a brand-new set of data every day to chew on and explore if you're interested—all those interactions with friends, family, colleagues, and strangers.

Reading *The Theory of Moral Sentiments*, you realize that morality and the meaning of life and how people behave haven't changed much since the eighteenth century. A wise-enough man can reach across more than two centuries, get your attention, and teach you a thing or two about yourself and what's important.

Adding to the delight is that Smith can really write. He's ironic, funny, and eloquent. When he hits his stride and warns you about getting too involved with fancy gadgets that fit in your pocket, you feel like you've found a secret source of wisdom. It's like discovering that Bruce Wayne, that successful man about town, has even more to share with the world and that his hidden side may be a lot more interesting than his public persona.

So why is *The Theory of Moral Sentiments* such a secret? Smith's road map to happiness, goodness, and self-knowledge is an old road map. The language is a little bit dusty, betraying its eighteenth-century origin. More than that, it's a road map that takes a lot of difficult twists and turns. The book occasionally doubles back on itself, and you find yourself in a spot you feel you've visited before. It isn't the easiest going for the modern reader.

Smith was writing an academic treatise, in intellectual competition with other authors with their own theories of human motivation. Most of those authors—writers like Bernard Mandeville and Francis Hutcheson and the Stoics—are long forgotten by most of us, along with their particular visions of humanity. Smith spends a decent amount of space explaining why his theories and insights are preferable to the competition's. So it doesn't read much like a self-help book.

It would make me very happy if more people read *The Theory of Moral Sentiments*. There's a wonderful edition still in print that is reasonably priced, and you can read it without charge at EconLib.org. Much of the charm of *The Theory of Moral Sentiments* is in the poetry of Smith's language. He was a great stylist, and that explains part of his success. But we twenty-first-century folk can find old prose daunting—the sentences are often long, and they're structured in ways our brains don't process well without some practice. They take a lot of time and patience. But if you're a little busy, part of my aim here is to give you Smith's insights and some of the best of his writing, just in case you don't get around to reading all of the original.

My other mission is to bring Smith's ideas into the present and see how they might be useful to you and me. We all see ourselves as special—and I'm sure you are—but we also have much in common. We have many of the same strengths and weaknesses. So when Smith teaches me something about myself, he often teaches me something about you. And that helps me treat you the way you'd like to be treated and gives you an idea of how to treat me. More than that, Smith was trying to understand what makes us happy and what gives life meaning. These are still pretty useful things to understand.

I struggled with how to get Smith's lessons into digestible form. The normal strategy would be to follow Smith's narrative in his book. But it's not a linear narrative, and many of his concerns and topics are not of interest to the modern reader. So I've taken Smith's most relevant insights and organized them into an order that I think is more accessible than the original. I also quote Smith directly whenever I can—I've managed to squeeze in most of my favorite quotes from *The Theory of Moral Sentiments*. But where necessary I've broken them up and offered running commentary explaining the allusions and stylistic peculiarities of a well-educated gentleman of 1759. Unless I note otherwise, all quotes are from *The Theory of Moral Sentiments*. Within those quotes, I will occasionally use brackets [like this] to explain an archaic word or phrase. I've left Smith's spelling as he wrote it. So "labor" becomes "labour," "honor" becomes "honour," and "befall" has only one "l."

You might be wondering what an eighteenth-century book on morality and human nature has to do with economics, Smith's most famous legacy. Behavioral economists today do their work at the border between economics and psychology, which is very Smithian territory. But most economists in the twenty-first century try to predict interest rates, suggest policies to reduce unemployment and soften its sting, or forecast the next quarter's GDP. Sometimes they try to explain why the stock market went up or down.

They're not particularly good at any of these things, and they often disagree on the best policies for getting the economy going. This leads noneconomists to conclude that economics is mostly about money and that economists are not very reliable predictors of the future or the best engineers to be steering the economic engine.

Unfortunately, what the media and the public expect from economists is what we are probably worst at—giving precise answers to questions that presume the economy is like some giant clock or machine whose innards can be mastered and then manipulated with some degree of precision. The failure of my profession to anticipate the Great Recession, to agree on how to get out of it, or to predict the path of the recovery should humble all economists.

But economics is actually quite useful—it's just not so useful for the things people typically expect from it. When I tell people I'm an economist, they often respond by saying something like "That must be useful around tax time," or "You must know a lot about the stock market." Alas, I am not an accountant or a stockbroker, I explain. But one very useful thing I've learned from economics is to be skeptical of advice from stockbrokers about the latest stock that's sure to skyrocket. Saving you from losses isn't as exciting as promising you millions, but it's still pretty valuable.

But the real point is that economics is about something more important than money.

Economics helps you understand that money isn't the only thing that matters in life. Economics teaches you that making a choice means giving up something. And economics can help you appreciate complexity and how seemingly unrelated actions and people can become entangled. These insights and others are sprinkled throughout *The Theory of Moral Sentiments*. Money is nice, but knowing how to deal with it may be nicer. A student once told me that a professor of hers said that economics is the study of how to get the most out of life. That may strike some of you, even those of you who majored in economics, as an absurd claim. But life is all about choices. Getting the most out of life means choosing wisely and well. And making choices—being aware of how choosing one road means not taking another, being aware of how my choices interact with the choices of others—that's the essence of economics.

If you want to make good choices, you have to understand yourself and those around you. If you want to get the most out of life, understanding what Smith has to say in *The Theory of Moral Sentiments* is probably more important than Smith's insights in *The Wealth of Nations*. Let's get started.

Chapter 2

❦

How to Know Yourself

You're sitting at your desk late in the afternoon, working on a spreadsheet for a proposal that has to get finished by tonight. At the same time, you're thinking about how to word the cover letter that will go with the spreadsheet. And somewhere even further in the back of your mind, you remember that your fourteen-year-old has a basketball game tonight and you're not sure how he's going to get there.

You're adding a column to the spreadsheet and wondering if your wife can take the kid to the game when a colleague pops his head into your office and asks if you've seen the news. Big earthquake in China, he tells you, tens of thousands are dead. Just as many missing. That's horrible, you reply. Your face shows the sadness you feel. Maybe you get on the Web to find more details. You think for a moment about the factory your firm has in China. Has it been hit?

You go back to the spreadsheet, five minutes go by, and your wife calls. She can go to the game after all and will take care of the car pool. She'll text you when your son scores and let you know how the game's going. That's great, you think to yourself—you'll be able to stay late and finish the proposal. It will be good to be home for dinner and not have that report hanging over you.

You've forgotten about all those dead Chinese.

Well, not exactly. You haven't literally forgotten. If a different colleague stopped by a little later and asked if you've heard the news, you'd say, sure, what a tragedy. Maybe with this second mention you'd think to make a donation to the Red Cross. And you might even make that donation.

But after a few minutes, even though you haven't literally forgotten about the Chinese, you won't be thinking about them. You'll be thinking about finishing the proposal and looking forward to dinner and hearing about your son's basketball game. And when your wife texts you that your son is playing well and his team is up by five at halftime, your pleasure in your son's achievement will not be diminished a whit by the thousands dead in China and all the families of the missing, desperate to find their loved ones. Their pain will struggle to penetrate your consciousness. Lying in the dark next to your wife, when she says, horrible, that earthquake, you'll grunt and agree and fall off to sleep without thinking about them for more than an instant. Your rest will be untroubled.

But imagine a different sequence of events. This time, when the colleague pops his head into your office, it's to tell you that a medical lab called. You know what it's about. There's a growth on your finger, and the call is about the biopsy. Your heart's pounding as you return the call. Cancer. That means the finger has to go.

It's not so bad. It's the little finger. Mastering the guitar will get a little bit harder, but that's OK. You don't even play the guitar. Not much of anything else will be affected, and the doctor assures you that no other treatment will be necessary. He's already lined up the procedure for tomorrow. That night, you lie in bed unable to sleep, anxious, afraid, and wishing that the whole thing was just a bad dream.

Writing in 1759, Adam Smith made the observation that we feel worse, much worse, about the prospect of losing our little finger than we do about the death of a multitude of strangers far away. That's human nature, the same in 1759 as it is today. Television and the Web make far-off tragedies more visceral than in Smith's time, but Smith's insight remains true. He starts by imagining the earthquake:

> Let us suppose that the great empire of China, with all its myriads of inhabitants, was suddenly swallowed up by an earthquake, and let us consider how a man of humanity in Europe, who had no sort of connexion with that part of the world, would be affected upon receiving intelligence of this dreadful calamity.

How would a man of humanity in Europe react?

> He would, I imagine, first of all, express very strongly his sorrow for the misfortune of that unhappy people, he would make many melancholy reflections upon the precariousness of human life, and the vanity of all the labours of man, which could thus be annihilated in a moment. He would too, perhaps, if he was a man of speculation, enter into many reasonings concerning the effects which this disaster might produce upon the commerce of Europe, and the trade and business of the world in general.

So yes, says Smith, we'll make a show of caring and express our sadness and maybe even wonder about the effects.

We'll make the right noises and the right facial expressions. But these are fleeting:

> And when all this fine philosophy was over, when all these humane sentiments had been once fairly expressed, he would pursue his business or his pleasure, take his repose or his diversion, with the same ease and tranquillity, as if no such accident had happened.

For better or worse, life goes on. Alas, Smith's assessment is generally true for most of us. Smith then imagines how differently we react to the potential loss of one's little finger:

> The most frivolous disaster which could befal himself would occasion a more real disturbance. If he was to lose his little finger to-morrow, he would not sleep to-night; but, provided he never saw them, he will snore with the most profound security over the ruin of a hundred millions of his brethren, and the destruction of that immense multitude seems plainly an object less interesting to him, than this paltry misfortune of his own.

Our ability to feel the pain of others is ever so much smaller than our ability to feel our own pain. I can handle that. But do we really care more about our little finger than we do about the death of an "immense multitude"? That's a little harder to accept. Smith seems to be saying that we are grotesquely self-interested.

This seems to confirm a commonly held view that Smith sees the world as driven by selfishness. Smith is often caricatured as a Scottish forerunner of Ayn Rand, who in addition to *Atlas Shrugged* wrote a book titled *The Virtue of Selfishness*. Smith spends a lot of time in *The Theory of Moral Sentiments* talking about various virtues. Selfishness does not make the cut.

What Smith does suggest in his famous book *The Wealth of Nations* is that people are fundamentally self-interested, which is not the same thing as selfish. At the very beginning of *The Wealth of Nations*, Smith explains the power of specialization in creating prosperity. Ideally, we specialize and get good at something, relying on the opportunity to get the rest of what we desire from others. But if we are all self-interested, why will my neighbor or a stranger help me out, providing the goods I cannot provide for myself? Smith's answer is a simple one—my neighbor will help me if there's something in it for my neighbor. Trading—offering something in return for my neighbor's help—is how we sustain the power of specialization. Here is Smith on the essence of trade, writing in *The Wealth of Nations*:

Whoever offers to another a bargain of any kind, pro-
poses to do this. Give me that which I want, and you
shall have this which you want, is the meaning of every
such offer; and it is in this manner that we obtain from
one another the far greater part of those good offices
which we stand in need of.

Smith continues with one of his most famous sentences:

It is not from the benevolence of the butcher, the brewer,
or the baker, that we expect our dinner, but from their
regard to their own interest. We address ourselves, not to
their humanity but to their self–love, and never talk to
them of our own necessities but of their advantages.

Few would disagree with this fundamental aspect of human nature. It can be hard to remember. So many students
show me letters that will accompany their job applications
that speak only of how much they've dreamed of working
for company XYZ and how much working for XYZ will
mean to them. They seem to think that their desire to work
for XYZ is sufficient to make XYZ desire them in turn. I
always encourage the students to address their employer's
self-love and not just their humanity—to come up with some
reason XYZ will benefit from hiring them. How would your
skills serve the goals of XYZ? Do you have any idea what

those goals are? The idea that other people care about themselves is generally a good thing to remember if you want them to do something for you in return.

But that's the job market, a pretty mercenary part of our lives. There are plenty of other situations in which we think about something other than ourselves. The very first sentence of *The Theory of Moral Sentiments* makes this point:

> How selfish soever man may be supposed, there are evidently some principles in his nature, which interest him in the fortune of others, and render their happiness necessary to him, though he derives nothing from it except the pleasure of seeing it.

We care about other people even when there's nothing in it for us. But how much do we care? Smith's example of the Chinese earthquake seems to be pretty consistent with a remarkably selfish view of human nature. But Smith isn't done. He asks: Suppose you could save your little finger by letting a few million Chinese perish. Would you do it? After all, you—like almost every real nonangelic, nonsaintly, merely human person I know—almost certainly finds the loss of a finger more disturbing to your happiness and general outlook on life than the deaths of millions who are far away. But if that's true, then you should be happy to let a million Chinese die to preserve your finger.

Yet no civilized person—no "man of humanity," as Smith describes him—would consider such an exchange for an instant. Smith writes that the mind recoils from even imagining such a bargain:

> To prevent, therefore, this paltry misfortune to himself, would a man of humanity be willing to sacrifice the lives of a hundred millions of his brethren, provided he had never seen them? Human nature startles with horror at the thought, and the world, in its greatest depravity and corruption, never produced such a villain as could be capable of entertaining it.

Hillel, the great first-century BCE Jewish sage of the Talmud, asked, "If I am not for myself, who will be for me? If I am only for myself, who am I?" Smith's answer is that if you are only for yourself, if you would save your finger by killing millions, then who you are is a monster of inhuman proportions.

So here is the second step in understanding yourself. Yes, you are profoundly self-interested. But for some reason, you do not always act in what appears to be your self-interest. Smith wonders how we reconcile our feelings with our actions:

But what makes this difference? When our passive feelings are almost always so sordid and so selfish, how comes it that our active principles should often be so generous and so noble? When we are always so much more deeply affected by whatever concerns ourselves, than by whatever concerns other men; what is it which prompts the generous, upon all occasions, and the mean upon many, to sacrifice their own interests to the greater interests of others?

Given our self-love, why do we so often act selflessly, sacrificing our own well-being to help others?

One answer would be that we are inherently kind and decent, filled with what Smith calls benevolence or what we moderns call compassion. We are altruistic; we care about others and hate to see them suffer. Yet Smith reminds us that losing our finger bothers us more than millions losing their lives. He rejects the argument that it is our benevolence or compassion that causes us to recoil from selfishly putting our own minor suffering ahead of the despair of millions:

It is not the soft power of humanity, it is not that feeble spark of benevolence which Nature has lighted up in the human heart, that is thus capable of counteracting the strongest impulses of self-love.

So if the milk of human kindness is in such short supply, why aren't we more outrageously selfish, more sordid? Smith's answer is that our behavior is driven by an imaginary interaction with what he calls the impartial spectator— a figure we imagine whom we converse with in some virtual sense, an impartial, objective figure who sees the morality of our actions clearly. It is this figure we answer to when we consider what is moral or right.

This impartial spectator sounds a lot like our conscience. But Smith's contribution is to provide an unusual source for that conscience. Smith doesn't invoke our values or our religion or any principles that might inform our conscience to produce feelings of guilt or shame at our misbehavior. Instead, Smith is saying that we imagine being judged not by God, and not by our principles, but by a fellow human being who is looking over our shoulder:

> It is reason, principle, conscience, the inhabitant of the breast, the man within, the great judge and arbiter of our conduct. It is he who, whenever we are about to act so as to affect the happiness of others, calls to us, with a voice capable of astonishing the most presumptuous of our passions, that we are but one of the multitude, in no respect better than any other in it; and that when we prefer ourselves so shamefully and so blindly to others, we be-

come the proper objects of resentment, abhorrence, and execration.

For Smith, the impartial spectator speaks to us in the voice of humility, which reminds us that we are little and the world is great:

> It is from him only that we learn the real littleness of ourselves, and of whatever relates to ourselves, and the natural misrepresentations of self-love can be corrected only by the eye of this impartial spectator. It is he who shows us the propriety of generosity and the deformity of injustice; the propriety of resigning the greatest interests of our own, for the yet greater interests of others, and the deformity of doing the smallest injury to another, in order to obtain the greatest benefit to ourselves.

Deep down, we know this is true. We know that we are small relative to the rest of the world. But we feel much of the time, maybe most of the time, as if we are the center of the universe. Call it the Iron Law of You. You think more about yourself than you think about me. There's a corollary to the Iron Law of You—the Iron Law of Me. I think more about myself than I do about you. That's just the way the world works.

Ever send someone an e-mail asking for a favor and he

or she doesn't respond? It's easy to forget that the recipient, like you perhaps, gets way too many e-mails to respond promptly. Your e-mail means more to you than it does to the person whose help you need. There's no reason to take it personally. When I don't hear back from someone, I assume that the person never received the e-mail in the first place. I resend it a few days later without mentioning (or complaining) that I sent it before.

I once sent a copy of one of my books to Tony Snow, then a columnist with *USA Today*. When I didn't hear back from him, I assumed he wasn't interested in writing about it. Then I found myself near his office; I stopped by to say hello. When I arrived, I was confronted with the Iron Law of You. The shelves that lined his office walls floor to ceiling were full of books. There were books piled on tables, books piled on the floor up to eye level, books everywhere. Books that people like me had sent in hopes of getting a mention in a column. I couldn't even tell if my book was there. He may have never received it. If he had, he may not have thought about it for more than an instant before putting it into a pile. Forgetting the Iron Law of You, I had assumed my book would arrive and be put in the center of a clean desk, begging to be read. In reality, my book was more like the ark entering the government warehouse at the end of *Raiders of the Lost Ark*.

The impartial spectator reminds us that we are not the center of the universe. Remembering that we are no more important than anyone else helps us play nicely with others. The impartial spectator is the voice inside our head that reminds us that pure self-interest is grotesque and that thinking of others is honorable and noble—the voice that reminds us that if we harm others in order to benefit ourselves, we will be resented, disliked, and unloved by anyone who is looking on impartially. If we are only for ourselves, it's not a pretty sight.

Smith rejects the idea that we do the right thing because we are compassionate and care for others in some abstract sense:

> It is not the love of our neighbour, it is not the love of mankind, which upon many occasions prompts us to the practice of those divine virtues. It is a stronger love, a more powerful affection, which generally takes place upon such occasions; the love of what is honourable and noble, of the grandeur, and dignity, and superiority of our own characters.

Self-love comes naturally to us. Loving our neighbor? Not so easy. Smith is saying that while we cannot love our neighbor as we love ourselves, we may be able at times to act as if we do. But the charitable actions we are capable of are not spurred by the same emotion that spurs us to protect ourselves and avoid pain and suffering. What spurs us to take care of our neighbor is the desire to act honorably and nobly in order to satisfy what we imagine is the standard that would be set by an impartial spectator.

I was once talking with a friend about God and morality. Does believing in God reduce your chance of committing a crime or a sin? What if you knew there was no chance of being caught—you're going to get away with a misdeed with certainty? So, on the surface, it's rational to steal or sin because no one is watching. My friend smiled and said that the whole idea of God is that He's always watching.

Smith's point is that *you* are always watching! Even if you're alone with no chance of being caught, even if no one knows you're stealing, you know. And as you contemplate committing the act, you imagine how an outsider, an impartial spectator of your crime, would react to your moral failure. You step outside yourself and view your actions through the eyes of another.

In the musical *Les Misérables*, Jean Valjean is a fugitive on the run. A look-alike of Valjean is arrested and is going to prison for a long, long time instead of Valjean. It's a glorious stroke of luck for Valjean—he'll finally be free. Tempted to let an innocent man suffer for his sake, Valjean asks Hillel's question, which is also Smith's question. Who am I? I am for myself, yes. But am I only for myself? In the song "Who Am I?" Valjean struggles with the urgings of self-interest— he can be free, but only by condemning another to the slavery of prison. Such selfishness is narrowly rational, of course; it's better to be free than in prison. But Valjean rejects the calculation. How could he face his fellow man if he should act so selfishly? How could he face himself? Only by turning himself in can he reclaim the Jean Valjean he wants to be.

Suffering to save someone else seems irrational. Smith is saying that the modern calculus of economics that looks at material costs and benefits alone is a flawed calculus. It's perfectly rational to tip in a restaurant that you'll never visit again, donate anonymously to charity, give blood without expecting to use blood in the future, and even donate a kidney without being paid for it. People who do those things do them gladly.

There is a long-standing debate in psychology and philosophy over whether our sense of morality is innate or learned. Many psychologists and philosophers argue that our brains are a blank slate, with everything imprinted by culture. Morality is all relative; it depends on where you grow up and how you are raised. In a recent book on moral psychology, *The Righteous Mind*, social psychologist Jonathan Haidt argues that there is a growing body of evidence that morality is more than just a culturally imprinted set of feelings. While Smith doesn't discuss the issue in these terms, his framework leans toward the innate view. Smith believes that our desire for approval from those around us is embedded within us, and that our moral sense comes from experiencing approval and disapproval from others. As we experience those responses, we come to imagine an impartial spectator judging us.

Whether or not honorable behavior is really motivated by people's imagining a watchful and judgmental impartial spectator, the concept gives us a powerful tool for self-improvement. Imagining an impartial spectator encourages us to step outside ourselves and view ourselves as others see us. This is a brave exercise that most of us go through life avoiding or doing poorly. But if you can do it and do it well, if you can hover above the scene and watch how you handle yourself, you can begin to know who you really are and how you might improve. Stepping outside yourself is an opportunity for what is sometimes called mindfulness—the art of paying attention instead of drifting through life oblivious to your flaws and habits.

All of us like to think of ourselves as good people. Even murderers can think highly of themselves and explain why their acts were justified. But if you want to actually be a good person rather than just impersonate one in your own mind, you should know what you're up against. You're up against the Iron Law of You—your inevitable self-centeredness, which not only wants to put you first, it wants you to pretend you're a good person even when you're not. Thinking of the impartial spectator—a coolheaded observer unaffected by the heat of the moment—can make you not only a better person, but also a more effective teammate at work, a better friend, a more thoughtful spouse.

Take the most basic human interaction—conversation. Everyone knows people who talk too much about themselves, hogging the conversation and taking more than their share of the airtime. It's harder to notice that sometimes you're that person. We like to talk about ourselves. We like to make our points. We have so much to say! How many times do you answer a question in conversation and wait for another instead of asking the person you're talking to about herself? How often do you listen for understanding rather than waiting for the other person to finish so you can make another point or tell another story? How would an imaginary spectator judge your conversational style? Imagining an impartial spectator can help you turn your conversation into more of a dance and less an exercise in taking turns—a dialogue rather than competing monologues.

When I first started podcasting in 2006, interviewing guests every week, I did more of the talking than I do now. I'd comment on my guest's observations, adding my own two cents after almost every response. Hey, I'm the host, I said to myself. People want to hear my views. And I have so much to say, don't I? Maybe. Sometimes. Certainly not all the time. I didn't need an impartial spectator to alert me; occasionally a flesh-and-blood listener would complain that I talked too much. I stepped outside myself and realized such listeners were right. The show got better when I made more room for my guests and let them do more of the talking.

Or consider how you react to slights and small injustices. Sometimes we feel an eagerness to indulge feelings of anger or resentment or injustice over petty annoyances it's better to ignore. Smith encourages us to step outside ourselves and ask whether someone watching would see us as more of a whiner than a crusader for justice. Rather than revving up our feelings of injustice, Smith is telling us a way to find serenity. Wag more, bark less.

The other day, my wife and I were in the car, and I mentioned that I'd rearranged a meeting so she and I could get together. That won't work, she said. Hadn't I read that e-mail she sent? The new time for the meeting conflicted with something I had to do for one of the kids. I *had* read the e-mail. But I'd forgotten about it when I rescheduled. I felt like an idiot. No problem, my wife said. Just re-reschedule the meeting—no big deal.

But it felt like a big deal. I was embarrassed to change the meeting yet again. I found my voice rising. In my eagerness to make my wife understand how bad an idea I thought it was to reschedule, I overreacted. Five minutes later, I thought of the impartial spectator. I stepped outside the situation. I'd treated my wife poorly. I sounded angry at her when I was really angry at myself—and embarrassed—for forgetting the e-mail. I apologized.

I wish I'd thought of that impartial spectator earlier. And had there been an actual spectator—a friend riding in the backseat, say—there's no way I'd have gotten so upset. A real spectator would have stilled my anger. Instead of being defensive, I'd have asked if there was a way to solve the kid issue without rescheduling, which is what we ended up doing.

Maybe you pay someone to cut your lawn or clean your house. Maybe you've hired someone to repair something that's broken. Maybe you're a manager with people reporting to you at work. It's hard to treat people the way they want to be treated—you're so busy; you have so many responsibilities. You like to think the people you work with will give you the benefit of the doubt if you're rude or inconsiderate. Would an impartial spectator see you as a kind and thoughtful boss or as falling short of the ideal?

If you want to get better at what you do, if you want to get better at this thing called life, you have to pay attention. When you pay attention, you can remember what really matters, what is real and enduring, versus what is false and fleeting. Thinking of an impartial spectator can help you know yourself and help you become a better boss, a better spouse, a better parent, a better friend. Thinking of an impartial spectator can help you interact with actual, real-life spectators and change how they think of you. That's nice, but Smith argues that it's more than a pleasant side benefit that comes from paying attention to how your behavior is perceived. It can actually lead to serenity, tranquillity, and happiness.

Chapter 3

ⱷ

How to Be Happy

You're nineteen years old, and your dream is to be a musician. Meanwhile, you're a sophomore at Stanford University. Making it as a musician is a long shot—and a Stanford degree is a good insurance policy. Your father, a very wealthy man, tells you he's going to give you your inheritance now, when it may be most useful to you. It's a small gift relative to your father's wealth, but it's still a lot of money—$90,000 worth of stock in your father's company. He tells you not to expect any more from him. This is it.

You can sell the stock and launch your music career. Or you can take a safer career path and hold on to the stock.

Your music career may thrive or flop. The stock may sky-rocket or crash. What should you do? Hard choice. Let's eliminate the uncertainty. I've seen the future, and if you sell the stock to finance your music career, the gamble will pay off. You'll achieve your dream. You'll be a successful musician. Not Louis Armstrong or Mozart, but a successful songwriter for television and films. You won't be a household name, but you'll be respected by your peers. You won't be a starving artist. You'll make a very good living. That's one path. And it sounds like a pretty good one.

In the second path, you give up on your dream of being a professional musician, stay in school, and hold on to the stock. With a Stanford degree you'll have a good career, just not the one you dreamed of. And you'll hold on to the stock as an investment. The stock will do well. Very well. To make it interesting, let's assume that if you hold on to the $90,000 worth of stock you're given as a nineteen-year-old, it will turn into $100 million over the next thirty-five years. You'll enjoy a lifestyle that will make your musician's salary look like a pauper's.

Which path is likely to make you happier? Should you follow your dreams or go with the big money? How much are you willing to pay to achieve your dreams? If you want to get the most out of life, which path do you choose?

Maybe being a musician isn't that exciting to you, so pick your own dream. What would give you enough pleasure that it would be better than being fabulously rich? Or maybe you can't think of anything. Maybe money is so appealing to you that you'd be thrilled to give up on your dream career, knowing that in return you'd have a life of incredible luxury.

Most choices in life aren't quite this dramatic. And most of us aren't anything like the son of Warren Buffett, the great investor whose company, Berkshire Hathaway, had a stock that really did grow a thousandfold over the last thirty-five years. Warren's son Peter Buffett actually took a chance on the music; he dropped out of Stanford at nineteen, sold the stock his father had given him, and asked his father for help with planning and budgeting in order to make that $90,000 last as long as possible. Four years went by. Peter Buffett scraped along, living in a small apartment and driving a beat-up car, trying, mostly unsuccessfully, to find paying work in the music business. Then he got a break. A neighbor introduced him to someone who needed music for an advertisement for a new cable television channel called MTV. One thing led to another, and Peter Buffett ended up with a successful career as a musician, which is no mean feat. He has written songs for movies and television and won an Emmy for his score for a TV documentary. He's had a meaningful life, doing something he loved.

Did he make the right choice?

Maybe that's an easy question for you to answer. Maybe not. As we'll see in chapter 5, Adam Smith was not a big fan of the pursuit of fame and fortune. His view of what we truly want, of what really makes us happy, cuts to the core of things. It takes him only twelve words to get to the heart of the matter:

> Man naturally desires, not only to be loved, but to be lovely.

The simplicity of this sentence is deceptive for two reasons. First, Smith uses words somewhat differently than we do, so understanding the phrase takes a little bit of work. Second, Smith packs a lot of richness into those twelve words.

The first part of Smith's summary of human desire—that people want to be loved—seems pretty straightforward, although Smith doesn't mean loved the way we mean it today, as connected to romance and family. He means it in a fuller sense. He means that we want people to like us, respect us, and care about us. We want to be appreciated, desired, praised, and cherished. We want people to pay attention to us and take us seriously. We want them to want our presence, to enjoy our company.

People do exist who claim not to care about what others think of them, but often it's a show, a form of protection from the possibility that they are not loved, not respected, and not appreciated. Often the people who appear not to care what others think about them are the ones who desperately crave approval. Most people want to be loved. And it comes to us naturally, Smith says; it's part of our essence. More than that, he says, "the chief part of human happiness arises from the consciousness of being beloved."

Smith also says it this way, emphasizing not just being loved but deserving to be loved, meriting being loved:

> What so great happiness as to be beloved, and to know that we deserve to be beloved? What so great misery as to be hated, and to know that we deserve to be hated?

When Smith wonders why people are unwilling to do things that are morally reprehensible, he invokes the impartial spectator—the idea that we're held in check by the judgments of an objective observer. Here, in talking about happiness, Smith invokes actual spectators, those in our social circle and beyond, who actually judge us. He's saying that when that jury of our peers loves us for what we do and who we are, we're happy.

You might rebel against Smith's formulation and argue

that it's unhealthy to be motivated by external approval. But Smith isn't arguing that our goal in life is to impress people around us so that we can be happy. That's the wrong way to be loved. For Smith, being loved is a natural result of being lovely. What does Smith mean by lovely?

In today's language, *lovely* means attractive to the eye or satisfying, as in "what a lovely vase" or "she sent me a lovely thank-you note." But when Smith says that we want to be lovely, he means worthy of being loved. A poor synonym would be *lovable*, but even that modern word conveys more emotion and less richness than what Smith has in mind. He's saying that we want to be seen as having integrity, honesty, good principles. We want to earn respect, praise, attention, and our good name—our good reputation—honestly. We want to be worthy of love. We want the love of others to be authentic in the sense that we don't receive it on the cheap. Smith is saying that we care about our reputation—how others view us—and we care that we come by that reputation honestly, that it mirrors who we truly are.

Here is the fullest expression of Smith's statement about being loved and lovely:

> Man naturally desires, not only to be loved, but to be
> lovely; or to be that thing which is the natural and proper

object of love. He naturally dreads, not only to be hated, but to be hateful; or to be that thing which is the natural and proper object of hatred. He desires, not only praise, but praiseworthiness; or to be that thing which, though it should be praised by nobody, is, however, the natural and proper object of praise. He dreads, not only blame, but blameworthiness; or to be that thing which, though it should be blamed by nobody, is, however, the natural and proper object of blame.

When we earn the admiration of others honestly by being respectable, honorable, blameless, generous, and kind, the end result is true happiness.

Loveliness is an end in and of itself. Think about marriage. You want to be a good husband, not because that means your wife will treat you well. You want to be a good husband because that's the right thing to do. Loveliness isn't an investment looking for a return. That's why you don't keep score in a good marriage—I did this for you, so now it's your turn to do something for me. I went to the grocery, so you have to run the kids to soccer. I was nice to you when you were under stress. Now I'm under stress, so you have to be nice to me. Or I'm up four to one, so the next three tasks fall on you. I went to two events with your friends, so for the next two, I drag you out with my friends.

If you think of your actions as a husband or wife as an investment or a cost-benefit analysis, you don't have a marriage motivated by love. You have a mutually beneficial arrangement. I can have that with my butcher or my baker. I don't want that arrangement with my wife. In a good marriage, you get pleasure from helping your spouse simply because that's the kind of partner you want to be—a lovely one. Better that than a contest to see who gets the better deal. My marriage isn't perfect. No one's is. But whenever I struggle with the challenges of all that a marriage entails, I learn the value of giving more, not less. I try being more lovely.

Smith's ideal is achieved when your inner self mirrors your outer self. Smith understood that we often fall short of the ideal. For years, financial adviser Bernie Madoff was seen by the outside world as a financial genius whose acumen and foresight improbably allowed him to earn consistently high returns for the investors who trusted him. Those returns seemed like a sure thing, and they were a sure thing as long as new investors could be found to feed his Ponzi scheme. Madoff was loved—revered—for what people thought was his wizardry as an investor. But Madoff knew that he was a fraud. He knew he wasn't lovely. His returns and promises came not from his ability and skill as an investor but from his ability and skill to deceive.

Then there's Warren Buffett, Peter's father, the "Sage of Omaha" and a man who actually appears to have legitimately good judgment, a man capable of growing a $90,000 investment into $100 million. Smith is saying that even before Madoff's Ponzi scheme was discovered, Buffett slept better than Madoff. Not just because he didn't have to worry about discovering new investors to cover up his fraud, as Madoff did, but because of Madoff's disconnect between his reputation and the reality. Smith is suggesting that Madoff was a less than happy man before he went to prison, not because he was afraid of being caught but because in his own eyes he was already caught; he was a failure, and he knew it even when no one else did. Madoff reportedly expressed relief when he was arrested.

Or think of Lance Armstrong vehemently denying that he had ever used performance-enhancing drugs. Year after year, his friends defended his reputation while Armstrong knew they were defending a lie. For a long time, he was very loved. But he was not lovely. It must have taken away some of the pleasure from the love he received. There was a disconnect between his reputation and the reality—and, again, not just because he worried about being caught. His public image was a lie, and it clashed with what he knew was the reality.

Smith realized that people are capable of fooling themselves, rationalizing or ignoring their imperfections and lack of loveliness. In the next chapter we'll look at self-deception and the challenges of self-awareness. But being loved and actually being lovely, rather than imagining you are, is the ideal.

A modern way to capture what Smith is talking about when he talks about being loved and being lovely is authenticity. We want to be real, and we want the people around us to be real in how they think about us. Respect or love or attention that is inaccurate because I don't deserve it isn't real. Someone who is thought to be lovely, but who knows he isn't, is living a lie.

So if I get praise I don't deserve, says Smith, it should bother me. The praise feels good. But knowing it is undeserved makes it impossible to enjoy, he says. Why? It's as if someone else is being complimented instead of you:

> The man who applauds us either for actions which we did not perform, or for motives which had no sort of influence upon our conduct, applauds not us, but another person. We can derive no sort of satisfaction from his praises.

Then Smith adds an insightful twist as to why it bothers us. It's not just the dishonesty of the compliment but that the compliment reminds us of what we might have done:

> To us they [his praises] should be more mortifying than any censure, and should perpetually call to our minds, the most humbling of all reflections, the reflection of what we ought to be, but what we are not.

So if someone praises me for my generosity because I volunteered for a community project that in fact I failed to help with, it's not just that the praise is inaccurate. It's also a reminder that I missed a chance to be generous. Undeserved praise is a reprimand—a reminder of what I could be.

Some, of course, are happy to ignore the reprimand and enjoy what Smith calls "groundless applause." Or worse, like Armstrong or Madoff, some try to create it dishonestly:

> The foolish liar, who endeavours to excite the admiration of the company by the relation of adventures which never had any existence; the important coxcomb [a conceited show-off], who gives himself airs of rank and distinction which he well knows he has no just pretensions to; are both of them, no doubt, pleased with the applause which they fancy they meet with.

Smith's reaction to those who indulge this impulse is scathing:

> It is only the weakest and most superficial of mankind
> who can be much delighted with that praise which they
> themselves know to be altogether unmerited. A weak
> man may sometimes be pleased with it, but a wise man
> rejects it upon all occasions.

To be loved without being lovely—to be praised without being praiseworthy—is a temptation for the weak and foolish person, not the wise one. Smith is encouraging us to strive for harmony between our inner self and our outer self. We may be tempted at times to be loved without actually being lovely. The wise man, says Smith, avoids that temptation.

By "unmerited praise" Smith means praise that is simply mistaken—my admirers thought I was someone who I am not. I know better, so ideally I correct the mistake. But there's another type of false praise I might be tempted to believe: flattery. Some flattery is just social pleasantry, such as paying someone a compliment. Another kind of flattery is insincere praise with an ulterior motive. Call it strategic flattery. Smith is providing a mechanism for explaining why flattery is so seductive. In Smith's terms, strategic flattery is an attempt by someone else to make me feel more loved than I deserve to be because the flatterer hopes to get something in return.

A friend of mine was offered a job as a high-ranking executive of a major health-care foundation, a foundation that gives away millions of dollars of grant money. When he accepted the job, another friend of his said, congratulations—you'll never pay for dinner again, and you'll never receive another honest compliment. I don't think he meant the part about never receiving an honest compliment literally. What he meant was that you'll have a hard time telling when you receive an honest compliment because you'll receive plenty of dishonest ones from people who will cater to your desire to be loved. Strategic flattery is fake love. Flattery can make someone feel loved who doesn't deserve it.

I always find it slightly awkward when students tell me they loved my class as they turn in their final exams. Some of them, maybe all of them, mean it. But it's striking to me how many of them say it before the exam is graded compared with the number who say it after the exam is graded. I'd like to believe that pattern holds because it's easier to find me in the classroom right after the exam, instead of a month after the class is ended. But some of it—how much I cannot know—is that the students, perhaps unconsciously, figure that if they can give me the gift of being loved, then I might feel some debt to them.

A friend of mine was the head of an organization for many years and got burned out. He decided to change his career and do something different, and he planned a transition to ease his successor into the leadership role. After the transition, he met his successor for coffee and asked him how it was going. Was he enjoying being the boss? Everything was fine, his successor said, but one thing bothered him. It seemed that his jokes had gotten funnier. His humorous asides, which once had caused mild amusement at the weekly meetings, provoked lots of laughter now that they were coming from the boss's mouth. His heart wanted to believe that he had become much wittier in the intervening time; his head told him otherwise.

We so want to be lovely that we can sometimes convince ourselves that we really did do what our friends think we did and that we really did have the right motives that they attribute to us. A boss can fool herself into thinking her jokes have gotten funnier when she became the boss; I can easily come to believe my class really is fabulous even after the exam is graded and the students are quiet, and my friend at the foundation handing out millions of dollars in grants can really believe that his control of the budget has nothing to do with why people keep asking if he has lost weight. ("You look fabulous!") Strategic flattery can succeed because we want to believe the compliments we receive are real. Once you realize the importance people place on being loved and lovely, you become a little better at detecting strategic flattery. And you're less likely, perhaps, to indulge in it yourself.

Our lives are filled with people who want to influence us in so many different ways. People around us want to be loved, just as we want to be loved. Sometimes they fool us into thinking we're something we're not, either for strategic reasons or just through an honest mistake. Smith encourages us not to be fooled. He encourages us to face ourselves honestly. But perhaps the biggest challenge we face isn't detecting false praise from others. Our biggest challenge comes from ourselves. We so much want to be lovely that we can convince ourselves of our loveliness when the reality is otherwise. The wise man may reject the praise he does not deserve. But it's so hard to be wise. And it's our own praise that's hardest to reject.

Chapter 4

❦

How Not to Fool Yourself

One of the happiest songs of my teenage years was "Pack Up Your Sorrows," a folk ballad sung by Richard and Mimi Fariña. Few people remember them today. A husband-and-wife folk duo, Richard was older than Mimi; she was only eighteen when they married, and he was twenty-six. When Mimi turned twenty-one, they celebrated with a big party in Carmel on the California coast. It was already a special day—Richard's novel, *Been Down So Long It Looks Like Up to Me*, had just come out, and he had done a book signing earlier. At some point during the birthday party, Richard Fariña climbed onto a motorcycle with a friend and went for a ride. The driver, his friend, lost control of the bike. Later, police said it had been going about ninety miles per hour on a tight turn. The driver survived the crash. Fariña flew into the air and was killed.

Richard Fariña was, by all accounts, an extraordinarily charismatic and talented human being. The unexpected death of such an exceptional man at such a young age would break the heart of not just his wife, but all those who were close to him. His wife's pain can be imagined only imperfectly. For it to happen while she celebrated her twenty-first birthday is beyond tragic. You need a darker, sadder word. I don't have one. Surely her friends rallied around her.

Mimi's sister—also a folk singer—was in Europe at the time, on a concert tour. Mimi, knowing the burden that crossing an ocean and a continent on short notice might impose on her older sister, told her she didn't have to come home for the funeral; she could come later and comfort her. Maybe Mimi really didn't need her sister to be there for her right away. Or maybe she felt like making the decision easier for her older sister.

How important is it to attend your sister's husband's funeral? Or the funeral of a friend's mother? There are always a hundred reasons to miss a funeral on short notice. Life is punctuated by choices like these, in which you have to choose between what is easy and convenient for you (finish your tour and enjoy the acclaim) and a chance to help those around you (go home and comfort your sister).

So many times we have to choose between what is pleasant or good for us and what an impartial spectator would see as the right thing to do. A consulting opportunity comes along that isn't as legitimate as you'd like—taking the job means betraying a principle using a measurement technique that you know is somewhat suspect. But maybe it seems like only a small betrayal—it's really no big deal, you tell yourself—and the opportunity is large. Or your boss asks you to do something you know isn't quite right or maybe even puts the company at some kind of risk, a risk that is real but difficult to measure; she's eager for your approval of an acquisition that promises quick profits, but the longer-term scenario looks very scary. Do you say something, or do you jump to the task?

What are you willing to give up in order to be lovely?

Then there are the smaller decisions we face. It's a Sunday morning, a little before lunch. I have time, if I hurry, to get to the gym and work out. That's what I want to do. But my son wants help on a math problem, my wife asks if I can run to the grocery, and my neighbor has just come home from the hospital and could use a smiling face at his bedside. I cannot do all of these activities. I may be able to do only one of them. What is the right thing to do?

I called these the "smaller decisions," but they are really not so small. Day by day, they add up to a life. How do we handle these choices? We want to be lovely. But being lovely can be hard—so hard that all of us know of times, maybe many times, when we fall short of the standard that an impartial spectator would demand or that we like to think we demand of ourselves. We often fail to live up to the ideals we champion and the principles we claim to embrace. How does Smith reconcile these failings, large and small, with his claim that we desire to be lovely?

One explanation for selfishness—or, worse, cruelty—is that some people don't imagine an impartial spectator, have no desire to imagine one, and in fact have no interest in being lovely. This is a tempting way to view our fellow human beings: people who don't act the way we think they should are immoral or evil.

But Adam Smith had a different idea of why we fail to live up to the standards an impartial spectator might set or the standards of the people around us whose respect and affection we'd like to earn: we are prone to self-deception. The impartial spectator whom we imagine and whose counsel we hear isn't quite as impartial as we'd like to think.

In the heat of the moment, when we are about to act, our self-love often overwhelms any potential role for the impartial spectator, "the man within the breast," our conscience:

> . . . the violence and injustice of our own selfish passions are sometimes sufficient to induce the man within the breast to make a report very different from what the real circumstances of the case are capable of authorising.

The imagined impartial spectator is an imperfect spokesperson for doing the right thing. Our urges can easily overwhelm our judgment. Afterward, once the moment has passed, we can reflect more calmly on our deeds:

> When the action is over, indeed, and the passions which prompted it have subsided, we can enter more coolly into the sentiments of the indifferent spectator. What before interested us is now become almost as indifferent to us as it always was to him, and we can now examine our own conduct with his candour and impartiality.

So in theory, at least, our reflection on our past behavior could lead to learning, self-knowledge, and a desire to behave differently in the future. In theory, we could resolve not to repeat the same mistakes we made in the past. Alas, Smith says we are not always "quite candid" when we reflect on our past behavior. An honest assessment of our behavior is often too hard to bear:

> It is so disagreeable to think ill of ourselves, that we often purposely turn away our view from those circumstances which might render that judgment unfavourable.

To rephrase Smith's original line about being loved and lovely, we want not only to be loved, we want to *think of ourselves* as lovely. Rather than see ourselves as we truly are, we see ourselves as we would like to be. Self-deception can be more comforting than self-knowledge. We like to fool ourselves.

Confronting our frailty and our failings can be too painful. So, yes, we avoid situations in which we are forced to confront our shortcomings. It's much more pleasant to delude ourselves. We are all cowards to some degree when it comes to self-awareness:

> He is a bold surgeon, they say, whose hand does not tremble when he performs an operation upon his own person; and he is often equally bold who does not hesitate to pull off the mysterious veil of self-delusion, which covers from his view the deformities of his own conduct.

By definition, a veil is mysterious. It hides one's face from the world. But I think Smith is saying that the veil of self-delusion is mysterious because it hides our visage from *ourselves*. It allows us to avoid seeing ourselves as we truly are. We may be overly sensitive to our physical deformities or even the slightest physical imperfections when we look in the mirror. Our eyes are drawn to those shortcomings the way a sore tooth attracts the tongue. But our moral failings? My failings as a husband, as a father, or a son or a friend? There is apparently no mirror for those. Most of the time, I'd rather not look.

The physicist Richard Feynman said, "The first principle is that you must not fool yourself—and you are the easiest person to fool." Who am I? Sometimes I'm the easiest person to fool. I'm so easy to fool, I can even convince myself that I understand how easy I am to fool. Other people— yeah, they're fooling themselves. But not me. No way. I see myself honestly. I see myself as I truly am. Believing that may be the biggest form of self-deception.

Smith's awareness of our inability to see ourselves clearly finds an echo in the modern literature at the intersection of psychology and economics called behavioral economics, a field that challenges the strict rationality of most modern economic models. Daniel Kahneman won the Nobel Prize in Economics for experimental work he did with Amos Tversky that examined how easily and often we misperceive reality. The co-winner that year was Vernon Smith, another experimentalist who studies how the mistakes people make individually can be tempered by their interactions with others in the marketplace. So while we may think our house is actually more beautiful than it is or our skills are more valuable than they really are, when we try to sell our house or look for a job, we gain a richer appreciation of how things truly are. I like to think Adam Smith would respect the work of both Kahneman and Vernon Smith and see them both as his intellectual heirs.

In modern times, some might argue that a little self-deception is a good thing; self-esteem, confidence, even if it's overstated, can be beneficial. Smith's view of self-deception, of overestimating one's merits, was decidedly negative:

> This self-deceit, this fatal weakness of mankind, is the source of half the disorders of human life. If we saw ourselves in the light in which others see us, or in which they would see us if they knew all, a reformation would generally be unavoidable. We could not otherwise endure the sight.

You aren't as lovely as you think you are. I'm not as lovely as I think I am. Our inability to face this reality, our desire to see ourselves as lovely, as more lovely than we truly are, keeps us from repairing our behavior. Self-deception makes us think we're lovely when we're not. Self-deception lulls me into thinking I'm virtuous when I am not.

Not surprisingly, we find it much easier to see the moral imperfections in others than our own shortcomings. Smith is warning us about that asymmetry. One way to correct that imbalance comes from the Baal Shem Tov, the great Jewish mystic and founder of the Hasidic movement, who died the year after *The Theory of Moral Sentiments* was first published. He said that we notice the flaws in those around us to remind us of our own flaws and to spur us to self-improvement. Our flawed neighbors are the mirror that allows us to see our own imperfections and ideally to remedy them. So when you see the annoyance of a co-worker over something trivial, instead of being surprised that he or she is so sensitive to so minor a slight, ask yourself if there are times when you get annoyed over something silly and unimportant. When your son is impatient, reflect on your own impatience and try to help your son by showing him you can control yourself.

Smith saw a similar role that those around us could play in improving our behavior. After describing self-delusion as mankind's fatal weakness, he notes that there is something that bolsters the potential impact of the impartial spectator:

Nature, however, has not left this weakness, which is of so much importance, altogether without a remedy; nor has she abandoned us entirely to the delusions of self-love. Our continual observations upon the conduct of others, insensibly lead us to form to ourselves certain general rules concerning what is fit and proper either to be done or to be avoided.

By *insensibly* Smith means unconsciously. We learn what is appropriate, and what is not, from the actions of others. Social norms and the general rules of morality that we learn from observing the world around us coach us as to what is admirable and what is not. Those general rules can mute our self-interested passions and give our conscience a fighting chance against our self-love. We see people choosing a path of behavior, and we notice how that behavior is judged by others. If it is judged negatively, that encourages us to avoid it. If it is judged positively, we are encouraged to engage in that action ourselves:

Other actions, on the contrary, call forth our approbation, and we hear every body around us express the same favourable opinion concerning them. Every body is eager to honour and reward them. They excite all those sentiments for which we have by nature the strongest desire; the love, the gratitude, the admiration of mankind. We become ambitious of performing the like; and thus naturally lay down to ourselves a rule of another kind, that every opportunity of acting in this manner is carefully to be sought after.

We also have natural, ingrained reactions to some behaviors that we view as either innately detestable or admirable. Smith uses the example of a murder by someone the victim trusted. We're horrified instantaneously without the need to see how others react. From this mix of natural reactions and lessons learned from experience we learn what is right to do. These norms are part of us—they help the imagined impartial spectator within us master the worst passions of self-love.

At Richard Fariña's funeral, an illustrious folksinger did end up attending and sang "Amazing Grace" in Richard's memory. But it wasn't Mimi's sister, Joan Baez, who sang that day. Joan decided to stay in Europe and finish her concert tour. Judy Collins was the singer.

The sisters Mimi Fariña and Joan Baez were partial spectators—that is, spectators with large emotional stakes in the matter. But you and I, dear reader, are impartial spectators. Do you think Joan Baez did the right thing by her sister and by her friend Richard when she stayed in Europe while her sister mourned? We probably don't have enough information to answer that question. But there is one more piece to their story that helped me more fully understand the mysterious veil of self-delusion.

When Joan Baez decided to stay in Europe, she reassured her sister that Richard would have wanted her to miss the funeral. By staying on tour she could honor his memory by playing some of his songs and talking about him. The decision to stay in Europe wasn't for herself. She was doing the right thing by poor Richard Fariña. And because Mimi loved Richard, Joan was even saying she was doing the right thing by Mimi. Evidently, Mimi didn't agree, though I don't know if she said so at the time. Decades later, in an interview with David Hajdu for his book on the 1960s folk scene, *Positively 4th Street*, Mimi said that Joan's estimate of Richard's desires wasn't quite right. She said that Richard would have preferred for Joan to have a nervous breakdown when hearing of his death and to be emotionally unable to continue her tour. I think Mimi was on to something.

Once you've noticed this strange logical inversion—what seems good for me is actually good for you!—you start to notice it more often. You can see it in daily life when you call someone who isn't as interested in your latest story as you are in telling it. "I'll let you go," they say. What they really mean is that they have to go. But they're getting off the phone in a way that makes it sound like they're doing you a favor. Then there's the football coach who quits because he wants to spend more time with his family. That urge usually lasts as long as it takes for another team to call with a job offer. Suddenly the coach has had enough time with his family and is ready to get back to his hundred-hour-a-week coaching job.

I used to think the reason people use selfless-sounding language to describe what are in fact selfish actions is to make others think they're selfless. It's a form of advertising. We want to be loved, so we couch our desires in a selfless form. We cloak our selfishness in something that looks more like kindness.

But Smith presents another possibility: we say these things not only to convince others but also to convince ourselves. We fool ourselves into thinking we're lovely when we're not. We do what's best for ourselves but convince ourselves that our motivation is for others. Joan Baez might really have believed that by skipping the funeral, she was doing what Richard Fariña would have wanted. We fool ourselves because we have such a powerful urge to consider ourselves to be lovely. Maybe Bernie Madoff did sleep as well as Warren Buffett—maybe he was able to convince himself that he was helping his "investors" make above-average returns. Maybe the charities whose funds he managed comforted him with what they were able to accomplish with the money he funneled their way.

According to Smith, our behavior sometimes falls short of our ideals not because we're bad people and not because our self-interest outweighs our benevolence, but because we don't realize we're not living up to our ideals. It's hard to say which idea is more depressing—that we fail to be lovely because we aren't lovely or because we've fooled ourselves into thinking we are. We not only hide our deformities behind the mysterious veil of self-delusion—we transform our deformities into virtues. That's how hard it is for us to face the impartial spectator.

So I not only fail to do the right thing. I not only fail to face my imperfection. I also convince myself that the wrong thing is the right thing. When my son asks for help with his math homework while I'm working on the manuscript of this book and I tell him I'm busy, I convince myself that by making this book better, it will be more successful and that will make it easier to send him to a good college. He doesn't really want me to help him with his homework, I tell myself—he wants me to finish my book. Ignoring his pleas for help isn't an example of me pursuing my self-interest. No—it's evidence of my selflessness.

Smith reminds us that it's hard to be objective when you have a horse in the race—your own self-interest. It's easy to convince yourself that you're doing the right thing when you're merely doing what benefits yourself. One way to protect yourself in such a situation is to seek out a mentor or a truly impartial real-life spectator who can help you see through the haze of self-love that so often blinds us.

A modern name for Smith's insights about self-deception is confirmation bias. Confirmation bias happens when we filter reality through our biases, ignoring evidence that challenges or refutes what we believe and eagerly accepting evidence that confirms what we believe. We like to think we're lovely, so we overemphasize and embrace memories that confirm our self-image while forgetting or misremembering anything that casts us in a less attractive light. We're biased about our own good nature. Because we want to see ourselves as lovely, we give ourselves the benefit of the doubt and then some, even sometimes transforming flaws into virtues.

But the challenge of seeing ourselves honestly extends beyond our interpersonal relationships. That's why I think Smith says that self-delusion is the "source of half the disorders of human life," and even then he may be underestimating the damage. We don't just fool ourselves about the quality of our personal behavior, limiting the true loveliness we might achieve in our relationships with friends and family. We fool ourselves about our worldview, our ideology, our religion, the evidence of our senses, and the interpretation of the world that we use to construct our beliefs. All the evidence we notice and remember confirms our views. Everything else is ignored or forgotten—or, better, dismissed based on flaws in the analysis. A reader of mine, Sam Thomsen, said it very well:

> The Universe is full of dots. Connect the right ones and you can draw anything. The important question is not whether the dots you picked are really there, but why you chose to ignore all the others.

Too often, that's what we do—we draw pretty pictures and ignore the missing dots, then congratulate ourselves on our artistry.

It's a big problem in my field of economics. Keynesians just know that Obama's stimulus package created millions of jobs. After all, their data and studies prove it. But somehow, the skeptics on the other side can prove the stimulus did little or nothing. Their data and studies seem just as convincing to them. How can that be? Both sides want to feel lovely and sure of themselves. So they manage somehow to convince themselves that the data on the other side of the argument are flawed or the studies are done by hacks or pawns of special interests.

Early in my career, I actually thought that the studies that supported my view of the world were the good studies. They were done carefully and thoroughly to establish truth. Those on the other side? They were easy to dismiss. Full of flaws. Bad assumptions. Incomplete analysis. As I have gotten older, I have become less confident and maybe more honest. The economy is too complex; we can't measure the interactions of all its various pieces with any precision. We don't have enough data, and we don't understand how things fit together. We are drunks looking for our lost keys under a lamppost not because that's where we lost our keys but because that's where the light is. We should be humbler and more honest. Our empirical studies are very imperfect. We often hold the views we do because of ideology and principle. Then we find some evidence that supports those views. We ignore the rest.

I once suggested at a conference for journalists that there was no empirical study using sophisticated econometric techniques that was so definitive that those on the other side of a contentious policy issue had no choice but to concede that they had been wrong. My point was that we all tend to think of ourselves as lovely and overvalue the evidence on our side while undervaluing counterevidence. No one likes admitting they're wrong. The journalists were skeptical. Was it really true? Weren't some studies so ironclad that they carried the day? I asked the other economists sitting around the room to see if they could come up with a counterexample. There was silence until finally one of them volunteered one of his own papers as a candidate—an obscure study of a not particularly contentious theoretical issue. I thanked him for making my point.

Of course, this too is a position I've become wrapped up in, making it harder for me to accept data or studies that might actually be definitive. But I believe such definitive studies are few and far between in contentious areas of economic policy, where there are so many factors affecting things that we cannot measure those factors accurately, if at all. F. A. Hayek, the great Nobel Prize–winning economist, called our overconfidence "the pretence of knowledge."

Another modern name for the challenge of understanding our complex world with any precision comes from Nassim Taleb—the narrative fallacy. We like narratives that follow a nice, clean pattern. Evidence that fits the narrative is noted after the fact. Other evidence that doesn't fit the narrative is discarded. Almost every day in the business section of America's newspapers and websites there's an article about the performance of the stock market that day or the day before. If the market went down, it's because of a discouraging report from the Bureau of Labor Statistics. Or the chair of the Fed said something that spooked investors. Or investors were "skittish" or "jittery" or "in the mood for profit taking."

The next day, the market goes up, and different explanations are invoked, sometimes by the same economists. But weren't investors skittish a mere twenty-four hours ago? Didn't the Fed issue a second statement similar to the one that spooked investors the day before? And wasn't there another disturbing piece of data from the Bureau of Labor Statistics?

How could the market go up when the same factors just caused the market to go down? Easy. Investors were tired of being skittish, the chair of the Fed wasn't as depressing as we thought she'd be, and that actually *lifted* investor spirits instead of depressing them. And, sure, the new Bureau of Labor Statistics numbers were depressing. But there was another set of numbers out of the Bureau of Economic Analysis that made investors optimistic. Of course the market went up! The world is a complex place. Everyone can explain why the stock market rose or fell yesterday. No one can predict what it will do tomorrow. It's all just ex post facto storytelling—the narrative fallacy.

I have no doubt that the economists quoted in these stories think they know what they're talking about. And the reporters think they're talking to experts. That's the power of confirmation bias and of Smith's insight into our unwillingness to remove that mysterious veil and confront who we really are—our unwillingness, like that of Smith's surgeon, to use the same rules on ourselves that we apply to others. We want to see ourselves as lovely. We all live some version of the narrative fallacy, censoring the parts of our life's story that we don't like seeing.

If you have water in your basement and ask a waterproofer for an assessment of the problem, he's likely to recommend spending $30,000 to dig a trench around your house and reset the piers that support your foundation. The guy who sells sump pumps will recommend a sump pump. The gutter guy will tell you need to replace your gutters, and the landscaper will want to construct a berm to direct water away from the house. When you have a hammer, everything looks like a nail.

You know these sellers make money by selling you stuff. But they aren't malicious, mustache-twirling exploiters of your naïveté. They're not scheming to make money off you.

They actually think they're helping you by swinging their hammer. They've come to ignore the possibility that there are other solutions to your problem that might actually be more effective or cheaper. They're sincere. Their sincerity makes them more effective and harder to resist.

We know that the gutter guy or the sump pump guy wants to make money off us, and that may make us more skeptical, even when they are sincere. But doctors, whom we tend to think of as caring and good-hearted, are no different. We all want to see ourselves as lovely. An ear, nose, and throat surgeon is more likely to think surgery is better than a nasal spray to fix congestion problems. She is less likely to remember that surgery doesn't always go as planned. There are unexpected side effects. There's uncertainty about whether the problem will actually get solved. There's uncertainty about how long the improvement will last.

In the nineteenth century, doctors eager to prevent women from dying in childbirth from puerperal fever would visit the autopsy table to examine recent victims, then hurry to the maternity ward for the next delivery. They didn't realize their germ-ridden hands were transmitting the disease. In Europe the death rate in the maternity wards of some hospitals was a terrifying one in six. Doctors like to think they are lovely. They must have found it unbearable to consider the possibility that they were the instruments of death. It was easier to believe there was something nasty in the air that was spreading the disease. The dramatically lower levels of puerperal fever in home births relative to hospitals must have been explained by something else.

Despite the efforts of Ignác Semmelweis to convince his colleagues that vigorous hand washing with disinfectant could eliminate the disease, better ventilation was still tried for years, even after Semmelweis proposed a theory of the disease and a preventive cure, and noted how death rates dropped when his ideas were followed. Semmelweis's personality may have made it harder for people to accept his theories. But surely part of the reason would have been understood by Adam Smith—it's no fun to believe that thousands of deaths could have been averted simply through better hand washing. The doctors didn't want to believe Semmelweis. It was too painful to consider.

Smith's insights into self-deception remind us of the limits of reason. Being aware of reason's limits doesn't mean being anti-reason or superstitious or irrational or even anti-science. Nassim Taleb points out that a map is very helpful for getting around Paris. But not if the map you're using is a map of New York. Using the wrong map unknowingly is worse than no map at all—it leads you to overconfidence that can be more harmful than confronting the reality that you're lost.

Scientists are human beings with their own limitations. Sometimes even the best quantitative analysis is worse than none at all because it gives the illusion of science, what Hayek called scientism. An awareness of reason's limits is a caution sign to remind us that we're not as smart as we think; we're not perfect truth seekers. We're flawed. Recognizing our flaws is the beginning of wisdom. Many things look like nails that do not benefit from being pounded. That should induce caution and humility for those with hammers.

Humility is an acquired taste. Once you come to like it, it's a dish best served hot. It's amazing how liberating it can be to say "I don't know." Maybe your intellectual opponents aren't evil. Maybe they see the world through a different lens or evaluate the evidence differently than you do. What seems like a decisive fact or study or piece of evidence usually can be answered by those on the other side. Hard as it is to imagine, your opponents have their own evidence that they find just as convincing. The world is a complicated place. Maybe there are more things in heaven and earth, Horatio, than are dreamt of in your philosophy.

The biggest challenge to applying Smith's insights on self-deception is the tendency to see those around you as blind to their own faults, overconfident in the research they champion, and unaware of the deep truths behind the worldview you champion. There is a temptation to say of all people besides yourself that *they* are the easiest people to fool. But it isn't so. Remember Feynman's insight: *you* are the easiest person to fool. Don't deceive yourself about your lack of self-deception.

Taleb, who has surveyed the territory of self-deception in a trio of books, quotes a Venetian proverb in his 2012 book, *Antifragile*: "The sea gets deeper as you go further into it." The more you know, the more you realize how much there is to know. You really don't have to pretend to know everything. Admitting ignorance can be bliss.

Smith alerts us to a flaw in our nature—our desire to be lovely can be so strong that we ignore any evidence to the contrary. We can fool ourselves into thinking we are lovely when we're not. But we don't just struggle to be lovely and to perceive ourselves honestly. Smith also argues that our desire to be loved has its own pitfalls.

Chapter 5

How to Be Loved

I imagine a rainy night in Edinburgh. I don't need a GPS to find Panmure House, the house that Adam Smith lived in for the last twelve years of his life and which is still standing. He greets me at the door and takes my wool coat, heavy with the rain, and welcomes me.

The stone house is cold and drafty. But there's a fire in the parlor, and that's enough to make the coldest house seem cozy. There are bookcases and books everywhere—about three thousand volumes. Many are bound in leather with an artistry that is rare in modern times.

Smith hangs my coat on the rack and moves the rack

closer to the fire to give the coat a chance to dry. He offers me a drink. I like to think it would be a glass of Laphroaig or Lagavulin, but those didn't come along until 1815 and 1816. But there's Bowmore, which is just fine. Adam Smith's drink of choice? In my mind's eye, Smith isn't much of a drinker. His mother is in the next room. He sticks to tea, while I sip my scotch from a small glass, struggling to decide what to ask the great man.

Being a gentleman, he'd sense my unease and draw me out. What are you doing in Edinburgh? he'd ask. I'd tell him that I came to see him, that I spend a lot of time just thinking about him and his ideas. Would he be surprised to still be of interest to an economist of the twenty-first century? I don't know, but I think the news would make him happy.

And that makes me wonder how he'd reconcile that reaction with what he has to say in *The Theory of Moral Sentiments* about happiness:

> What can be added to the happiness of the man who is in health, who is out of debt, and has a clear conscience?

I imagine him uttering those words, accompanying them with a sigh and maybe just the slightest shake of his head. It's a rhetorical question, after all, and the answer he expects in response is "Very little." And all throughout the book, Smith makes it abundantly clear that money and fame don't lead to happiness. What leads to happiness is being loved and being lovely. Money and fame just don't seem to fit into that equation.

For much of Smith's life, he had his health, he had no debts, and as far as we know, he had the clearest of consciences. But he had so much more. The publication of *The Wealth of Nations* brought him money and renown in his lifetime. Even *The Theory of Moral Sentiments* brought him a little of both as well. Did that not add to his happiness?

He couldn't have known of the immortality that awaited him, but he must have suspected that he might be remembered past his death. Wouldn't that cheer him up more than a little?

Wouldn't being world-famous or just a little bit rich add to one's happiness? Wouldn't Smith himself get pleasure from knowing he's become somebody, and not just any somebody, but a big-time somebody in the world of economics and public policy? More famous than his good friend David Hume, one of the greatest philosophers. More famous than his contemporary Voltaire, who ushered us into the age of reason. More influential, maybe, than both of them. Would it quicken his pulse or gladden his heart to know that late in the twentieth century, over two hundred years after he wrote *The Wealth of Nations*, a prime minister of the United Kingdom would carry it around in her purse? Wouldn't knowing how loved he had become for his loveliness add to his happiness?

How about you? What, if anything, would add to your happiness? Would you like a little more money or a little more renown? Would it make you happy? Would you grovel to get a better-paying job? Or take a higher-paying job that deadens your soul? Would you do a job that requires deception or fraud for you to succeed? Would you spend less time at home—less time with your family—if it meant getting a modest raise? What if that meant jeopardizing your marriage or how your children grow up? What if it meant a big raise, a big promotion, or fame and glory? Or power? Would that make it OK to put your career first and your family second? How important is money or professional success to our happiness?

An NFL coach may pretend he's quitting to spend more time with his family, but his choice to go back to work when a new team calls tells us what he really values. Only thirty-two people can be an NFL coach at any one time. So they work hard to try to find an edge that will let them win an extra game or two and keep their jobs. They work a hundred hours or more each week. They fall asleep in the office watching film of an upcoming opponent and wake up early to watch some more. When you work a hundred hours a week you can't give your kids even quality time, let alone quantity time. Is it worth it? At least thirty-two men seem to think so. Myriad more wait to take their place should they falter. Those in waiting are eager to give up spending time with their families for the combination of money and fame that comes with being an NFL coach. Are they making the right choice? Or are they fooling themselves about the satisfaction they'll get from achieving the heights of professional success? Is Adam Smith right about what we really care about?

Look at people who want to be president of the United States. The candidates always show us pictures of themselves with their loving families, suggesting they care about their family as much as the rest of us do, perhaps more. But they certainly don't spend much time with them. They can't. Campaigning for office is a full-time job and then some. Is it worth it? Those who choose to do it seem to think so.

I was fourteen years old when Jacqueline Kennedy remarried and became Jackie Kennedy Onassis. I was puzzled by the marriage. Why, I asked my father, would Jackie Kennedy marry Aristotle Onassis, a physically unattractive man who was twenty-three years older, especially after being married to the young and handsome Jack Kennedy? My father's answer was simple—Onassis has a lot of money. But, Dad, I protested. Jackie Kennedy comes from a wealthy family. She married into the Kennedy family, which is extremely wealthy. She's already rich. It's nice to be rich, my Dad explained. But it's nicer to be even richer. It's nice to visit a beautiful tropical island. It's more fun to own it. It's nice to fly first class. It's nicer to have your own airplane. A big diamond ring is nice. A bigger one is even nicer. Aristotle Onassis was worth $500 million when he died. That's a lot of islands and planes and diamonds.

I don't know if my dad was right about what motivated Jackie Kennedy. But he was on to something. People do generally prefer having more wealth and a higher income compared with what they already have. They certainly act as if money is the source of happiness and that more money means more happiness. Something inside us drives us to want more. Something else inside us tells us that more isn't necessarily better. Something else inside us makes us wonder if the price of wealth is worth paying.

I have a friend with an incredibly demanding job that he doesn't particularly enjoy. But he puts up with it because he makes a lot of money, much more than he could make working for another company or doing something else. He has high blood pressure. His children get older every year.

He complains about the stresses of his life and asks for my advice. Quit your job, I tell him. Earn less money. Spend more time with your wife and kids. Be happier. I can't, he says. I have all these big deals in the works. Let me win those contracts, bag those bonuses. Next year I'll quit and slow down. But when next year comes along, he tells me about the new deals and the new bonuses. Next year is always a year away. He reminds me of the bar with the permanent sign—free beer tomorrow.

Every year his salary grows. Every few years he moves into a bigger house and gets a new car. Is he happier? Evidently not. Despite the larger salary and the bigger house and the nicer car, he's not content. Just one more year. Then he'll have enough, he says.

There's a little of my friend in all of us. Sometimes money seduces us and encourages us to do things we know deep down aren't what we really want. A lot of ink has been spilled reminding us that the rat race is run by rats. But sometimes the rat inside us takes charge, and we find ourselves running the maze, looking for a bigger piece of cheese.

Smith says we naturally desire not only to be loved but also to be lovely. How does he reconcile this claim with what seems to be what we really desire—fame and fortune? Aren't those the two urges that drive us?

Smith has an answer, and to get to it, we need to understand just how negative he is about ambition and the drive for fame and fortune. Let's start with the fortune part.

In *The Theory of Moral Sentiments*, Smith recalls a story from Plutarch's *Lives* that may shed light on my friend's inability to quit his job. It's the story of Pyrrhus, the king of Epirus, a region of Greece. Pyrrhus is planning an attack on Rome. His trusted adviser, Cineas—Smith him calls the king's "favorite"—thinks it's a bad idea. Cineas is an impressive guy, a brilliant wordsmith and negotiator whom the king often uses to represent himself. But even though he has the trust and ear of the king, it's usually not a great idea to tell the king he's making a mistake, even when you're a favorite of his, so Cineas takes a roundabout approach. Here's how Cineas begins in Plutarch's version:

> "The Romans, sir, are reported to be great warriors and conquerors of many warlike nations; if God permits us to overcome them, how should we use our victory?"

Well, says Pyrrhus, once we conquer Rome, we'll be able to subdue all of Italy. And then what? asks Cineas. Sicily would be conquered next. And then what? asks Cineas. Libya and Carthage would be next to fall. And then what? asks Cineas. Then all of Greece, says the king. And what shall we do then? asks Cineas. Pyrrhus answers, smiling:

> "We will live at our ease, my dear friend, and drink all day, and divert ourselves with pleasant conversation."

Then Cineas brings down the hammer on the king:

> "And what hinders Your Majesty from doing so now?"

We have all the tools of contentment at hand already. You don't have to conquer Italy to enjoy the fundamental pleasures of life. Stay human and subdue the rat within. Life's not a race. It's a journey to savor and enjoy. Ambition— the relentless desire for more—can eat you up.

Plutarch's *Lives* was written about two thousand years ago. Plutarch was telling a story from maybe three hundred years earlier. That money doesn't make you happy is an old story. The fundamental things in life apply as time goes by. Here's a modern riff on the same theme. You can find various versions on the Internet. Smith (and Plutarch) would have loved it.

An American businessman was at a pier in a small coastal Mexican village when a boat with just one fisherman docked. Inside the small boat were several large yellowfin tuna. The American complimented the Mexican on the quality of his fish and asked how long it took to catch them. Not long, was the reply. The American then asked the Mexican how he spent the rest of his time.

"I sleep late, fish a little, play with my children, and talk with my wife. I stroll into the village each evening, where I sip wine and play guitar with my friends. I have a full and busy life."

The American replied, "I have an MBA and can help you. You should spend more time fishing and, with the proceeds, buy a bigger boat. With the proceeds from what you could bring in with the bigger boat, you could buy several boats; eventually you would have a fleet of fishing boats. Instead of selling your catch to a middleman, you would sell directly to the processor, and eventually open your own cannery. You would control the product, processing, and distribution.

"You would need to leave this small village. Move to Mexico City, and then maybe to Los Angeles, where you will run your expanding enterprise."

The Mexican fisherman asked, "How long will this all take?"

The American replied, "Fifteen or twenty years."

"But then what?" asked the Mexican.

"That's the best part! When the time is right, you

could go public. You'll become very rich; you would make millions!"

"Millions?" replied the Mexican. "Then what?"

The American said, "Then you would retire. Move to a small coastal fishing village where you would sleep late, fish a little, play with your kids, spend time with your wife. In the evenings, you could stroll to the village, where you could sip wine and play your guitar with your friends . . ."

When a story from 2,300 years ago is retold by a great philosopher-economist two hundred years ago and then recast in the present about an MBA and the seeming pleasures of going public, it probably has some transcendent meaning. I don't know what's more remarkable, the fact that the message keeps getting preached or that we haven't absorbed its lessons despite all the retellings. Something keeps pushing us forward. Maybe the preachers are just wrong. Maybe we really will be happier in a bigger house, driving a nicer car, and having a fancier phone.

Adam Smith said no—things don't make us happy. But at the same time, he understood the seductive appeal of toys and gadgets. Though he lived two centuries before Apple's founder Steve Jobs, Smith understood the weird sensation that you are missing out because you don't have the new iPad with Retina display or a lime-green magnetic cover or a video camera. My iPad—the first model—doesn't even have a camera that takes still shots! I should upgrade, don't you think?

Every Sunday my newspaper brings me ads for a bigger TV than the one I have. When I go to Costco, those giant TVs are at the front of the store, a gauntlet I have to pass through to reach the superb produce and the oversized olive oil, mustard, and ketchup. My TV is maybe five years old, and when I compare it with the ones I encounter in the ads or at Costco, it starts to look like my old 20-inch that I replaced with its newer, big-screen cousin.

This is life in the modern world. Within weeks or months of having the latest, coolest, most beautiful device, it's out of date. Human creativity advances at such a breakneck pace, the device that made your heart sing just a few months ago now looks like an antique.

I want the new one, the faster one, the thinner one. But once I get it, does anything change? Sometimes. My iPhone gives me a lot more satisfaction than my first cell phone gave me. And nearly infinitely more delight. That's not surprising. What's surprising is how much I want the newer one even when I know that many or most of its features really aren't that much better than what I have now. But I want them anyway. And, oh, how we take these devices for granted once we have them. I can still get annoyed when I'm on a call in the car or on the train and I hit a dead zone. How can that annoy me? Why isn't the marvel that my cell phone works at all enough to keep me rapturous about its mere existence?

What gadgets and toys were available in 1759? Smith writes of a "tooth-pick, of an ear-picker, of a machine for cutting the nails, or of any other trinket of the same kind," things that can be carried in a tweezer case, the man-purse of the eighteenth century. I shudder to think of using an ear-picker, even a fancy one. And a "machine for cutting the nails"? A nail clipper must have been a pretty useful improvement over a knife.

Smith couldn't imagine a twenty-first-century machine—a robot on an assembly line, or an electric razor. But his insights into technology are surprisingly prescient. He understood the human desire to make life easier, better, faster. And he also understood the seductive appeal of machines, and that ear pickers and nail clippers may not always deliver on their promise of excitement and novelty. But we want them anyway, and we look for ways to make them more effective and more elegant.

You might argue that an eighteenth-century nail clipper

cannot possibly be compared to your iPod nano or the 16-megapixel camera you can slip into your pocket. But the psychological appeal of devices in either time is pretty similar. We're living in a technological age, but maybe that age started a lot longer ago than we think.

One of Smith's insights about technology and gadgets is that we often care more about the elegance of the device than for what it can achieve. He gives the example of a watch that loses two minutes a day, likely a common occurrence in the eighteenth century. Smith says the owner of such a watch might get rid of it and pay a premium for a watch that is dramatically more accurate. But, Smith complains, the owner of the better watch may not be any more punctual than he was with the timepiece that performed more poorly. He bought the better watch simply because it is a superior gadget, not to make his life any better:

> But the person so nice with regard to this machine, will not always be found either more scrupulously punctual than other men, or more anxiously concerned upon any other account, to know precisely what time of day it is. What interests him is not so much the attainment of this piece of knowledge, as the perfection of the machine which serves to attain it.

Then Smith really opens fire on the gadget lovers:

> How many people ruin themselves by laying out money
> on trinkets of frivolous utility? What pleases these lovers
> of toys is not so much the utility, as the aptness of the
> machines which are fitted to promote it. All their pock-
> ets are stuffed with little conveniencies. They contrive
> new pockets, unknown in the clothes of other people, in
> order to carry a greater number.

"All their pockets are stuffed with little conveniencies"
is a perfect description of the modern business warrior, who
will often carry in his pockets an iPhone for his personal
use, a BlackBerry for his work e-mails, his wallet, his ear-
buds or Bluetooth headset, a pen (just in case), his keys, a
thumb drive, and maybe a small camera. He longs to have
a pocket big enough to carry his Kindle or iPad mini.
Women at least have a purse for their collection of "little
conveniencies." Most men are stuck with just their pockets.
I don't know if anyone buys them, but there are (or at least
were) vests you can buy with specific pockets for carrying
your iPad, two types of cell phones, and all the rest of the
usual modern business paraphernalia.

Smith was certainly on to something about the aesthetic
appeal of gadgets relative to what they actually can achieve.

I have at least three apps on my iPhone that map the stars when I hold my iPhone up to the sky. I use them infrequently, maybe a few times a year. I certainly don't need three. But their beauty moves me. I'll notice something in the night sky that looks too bright to be a star. It must be a planet. Which one? I wonder. I open one of the astronomy apps on my phone and lift my phone to the sky. It's Jupiter. Why do I care? I don't know. Knowing that I am looking at Jupiter has no apparent usefulness. But there's something sublime about knowing, and I get an independent pleasure that my phone can somehow let me know that it's Jupiter and not Venus.

I have an app that lets me explore what purports to be the actual DNA sequence of the CEO of a DNA-sequencing company. There's no use for it at all. I just want to marvel that it can be done and that I can hold the results in the palm of my hand. I have so many apps that I looked at for five minutes; I delighted in their elegance and never opened them again. I bought them because they're beautiful and someone had figured out how to make them work.

Maybe Smith goes too far. Yes, the desire for the latest, hippest gadget can be seductive and destructive. But some of my devices, the gadgets I love the best, do their job extraordinarily well. So yes, I've owned four different cameras over the last eight years, moving up with each purchase to what I hoped was a better camera that would do a better job. But I didn't just admire how small they were or how well designed they were. Their small size meant I carried my camera more often. Their design improved the quality of my pictures. The result is the thousands and thousands of pictures they let me take and share.

The real problem I have with my gadgets is keeping them from taking over my life. Just keeping their batteries charged and keeping track of the chargers and cords and cases is time-consuming enough. But the real challenge is the temptation to spend too much time in the virtual world rather than the real one, compulsively seeking the modest dopamine rush of a new e-mail or three versus connecting in a more vivid way with the human being next to me. I'm not alone. You go to a party and the guests are hunched over their smartphones. There's the sports fan who checks the progress of his fantasy football team every thirty seconds at a Sunday brunch, and the person who buys his iPad as a reading device but ends up playing games on it for hours. So there are benefits to modern gadgets Smith could not have imagined in his world of ear pickers and tweezer cases, but there are costs as well.

Smith understood two centuries ago that gadgets and

devices signal our status and wealth. That's another reason, apart from their utility, that we want the latest, hippest, shiniest phone, car, and toy. It's a way to signal to the world who we are, or at least who we sometimes think we are—our ranking in hipness and material success. Smith blamed ambition for our urge for the newest device and the false belief that newer equals happier:

> The great source of both the misery and disorders of human life, seems to arise from over-rating the difference between one permanent situation and another.

The grass on the other side of the fence often appears greener. We imagine we'd be happier if only we were richer or more famous or had a better job. Greed, ambition, and vanity are how Smith characterizes the vices that push us toward dissatisfaction with what we already have. Just one more deal. Just one more year in this lousy job. Just one slightly cruel act to get ahead of a co-worker and get that promotion. Smith calls these vices "extravagant passions," and he warns us of their power.

> Some of those situations may, no doubt, deserve to be preferred to others: but none of them can deserve to be pursued with that passionate ardour which drives us to

violate the rules either of prudence or of justice; or to corrupt the future tranquillity of our minds, either by shame from the remembrance of our own folly, or by remorse from the horror of our own injustice.

The first part of that sentence is the key to Smith's attitude toward money, financial success, ambition, and ego:

Some of those situations may, no doubt, deserve to be preferred to others: but none of them can deserve to be pursued with that passionate ardour which drives us to violate the rules either of prudence or of justice;

For Smith, money and fame should be kept in perspective. He concedes that most of us will always prefer having more money to having less. Public recognition is pleasurable. But don't be consumed by the desire to consume or a passion for public acclaim. You'll end up violating the rules of prudence or justice.

By justice, Smith means the virtue of not injuring or harming others. By prudence, Smith means the virtue of taking care of oneself using both foresight—looking down the road to assess the consequences of our action—and self-control, the ability to give up something today in return for a greater gain in the future:

The qualities most useful to ourselves are, first of all, superior reason and understanding, by which we are capable of discerning the remote consequences of all our actions, and of foreseeing the advantage or detriment which is likely to result from them: and secondly, self-command, by which we are enabled to abstain from present pleasure or to endure present pain, in order to obtain a greater pleasure or to avoid a greater pain in some future time. In the union of those two qualities consists the virtue of prudence, of all the virtues that which is most useful to the individual.

Smith sees nothing wrong with what we moderns call success. It's the *passionate* pursuit of success that corrodes the soul, in Smith's view. Certainly a relentless pursuit of money and fame can ruin your life. But if the gadgets and material success that come with money can be so destructive, why do we pursue them so zealously? And if they rarely make us much happier, if at all, why take the chance? How does Smith explain our pursuit of so many unhealthy goals?

One answer is that we are simply mistaken or ignorant—we think that being rich and famous will indeed make us happy. But Smith sees something more pernicious at work, and it comes from our desire to be loved and lovely. Remember that Smith uses the word *loved* to encompass not just romantic love. When he says we want to be loved, he means paid attention to, liked, respected, honored. We want to matter. We want people to notice us, to think highly of us.

Smith notes that the world pays attention to rich and famous and powerful people and not necessarily to wise and virtuous people:

> ... upon coming into the world, we soon find that wisdom and virtue are by no means the sole objects of respect; nor vice and folly, of contempt. We frequently see the respectful attentions of the world more strongly directed towards the rich and the great, than towards the wise and the virtuous.

We sometimes think celebrity is a modern invention chronicled by *People* magazine and propagated through cable television or YouTube. Certainly, we moderns have a special flair when it comes to celebrity. More and more people get fifteen minutes of fame, and the durable celebrities—the movie stars and singers and athletes—have a level of exposure that is unparalleled. But there is nothing new under the sun, as the author of Ecclesiastes understood long ago. The obsession of the masses with the rich and famous is a very old phenomenon.

Much of Leigh Montville's biography of Ted Williams is a meditation on what celebrity was like in the 1940s and 1950s. And it turns out to be not much different than it is today. Even without multiple ESPN channels on cable television, and even without talk radio, athletes were still very different from the rest of us in a way that's hard to fathom.

Montville tells the story of the time that Jimmy Carroll, a friend of Williams's, borrowed Williams's car, a distinctive Cadillac Coupe de Ville, for a date. Carroll and the date pulled into the parking lot of a restaurant and were confronted by a policeman. What was Carroll doing driving Ted Williams's car? It turned out that all the cops in Boston knew the car. After Carroll convinced the policeman that he wasn't a thief, the policeman had one more question. Could he sit in the car while Jimmy and his date had dinner? Sure, Carroll said. When Carroll came back out to the car, there were six policemen sitting in Ted Williams's car. The first cop had called five buddies to share the thrill.

What *was* the thrill, exactly? How can celebrity transform an inanimate object into a glamorous object of desire? It's one thing to love your watch for its accuracy even when you don't care about being on time. But to love sitting in a car because someone famous has sat there before you and will sit there after you? Is it because you're doing something few others are able to do? Is it because it somehow links you to someone who is gloriously skilled? Or is it a function of being one degree of separation from someone who is that loved, that adored, that admired? No doubt part of the thrill is being able to tell someone you sat in Ted Williams's car. But why does anyone care?

Something inside us reveres those who are revered. We idolize those who are idolized. We love those who are loved. Part of it is an awe for excellence. We will watch astounding feats on the Internet simply because they're astounding and we can't imagine how they can be done, even when they are no more practical than solving a Rubik's Cube. We will watch and admire expertise that has no practical purpose. After all, the ability to hit a baseball moving unpredictably at one hundred miles an hour with a wooden stick is really not practical at all. A great heart surgeon would seem to be more admirable. But no one wants to sit in the car of a great heart surgeon unless that heart surgeon is world renowned, and maybe even that isn't enough. No heart surgeon reaches the reach of LeBron James. There is something ineffable about fame that draws us to it. Maybe Smith's insight into our desire to be loved is part of the answer. Somehow, being near people who are loved is exhilarating.

Celebrity was addictive in 1940. And it was addictive in 1759 in a world without television, radio, or YouTube.

Smith's insights into the celebrities of his day are just as timeless as his insights into money and gadgets. Who were the celebrities of Smith's day? Many were nobility or the hangers-on at court, people who had inherited money and notoriety or who curried favor with the nobility. Some were his contemporaries. Others he knew from history. He didn't think much of those who achieved fame simply by currying favor with the great and powerful. In his view, they lived in a world devoid of true loveliness:

> In the courts of princes, in the drawing-rooms of the great, where success and preferment depend, not upon the esteem of intelligent and well-informed equals, but upon the fanciful and foolish favour of ignorant, presumptuous, and proud superiors; flattery and falsehood too often prevail over merit and abilities.

For Smith, the pursuits of money, fame, or power were all part of the same temptation—various paths to being loved, paths to being relevant and noticed by others. It is the attention paid that motivates people to seek wealth:

> The rich man glories in his riches, because he feels that they naturally draw upon him the attention of the world, and that mankind are disposed to go along with him in

all those agreeable emotions with which the advantages of his situation so readily inspire him.

It's all about the ego and not what money, fame, and power actually bring:

At the thought of this [the attention of the world], his heart seems to swell and dilate itself within him, and he is fonder of his wealth, upon this account, than for all the other advantages it procures him.

Writing about famous people, people he calls men of "rank and distinction," Smith explains why people want to be famous and why the rest of us pay attention to them:

The man of rank and distinction, on the contrary, is observed by all the world. Every body is eager to look at him, and to conceive, at least by sympathy, that joy and exultation with which his circumstances naturally inspire him. His actions are the objects of the public care.

We "conceive, at least by sympathy, that joy and exultation with which his circumstances naturally inspire him." What Smith is saying is that we live vicariously through the famous. Using our imagination, we put ourselves in their shoes and get a taste of what they must be feeling—their joy and exultation, emotions that we imagine accompany their nearly perfect life.

One of the ways the rich and famous are loved is that people pay attention to their pronouncements even when there is little or no expertise or understanding behind them. We listen anyway. We can't look away:

> Scarce a word, scarce a gesture, can fall from him that is altogether neglected. In a great assembly he is the person upon whom all direct their eyes; it is upon him that their passions seem all to wait with expectation, in order to receive that movement and direction which he shall impress upon them; and if his behaviour is not altogether absurd, he has, every moment, an opportunity of interesting mankind, and of rendering himself the object of the observation and fellow-feeling of every body about him.

"If his behaviour is not altogether absurd"—meaning we'll put up with a lot of misbehavior and a pretty significant amount of absurdity and still be riveted by the latest rock star or movie star.

According to Smith, in the eyes of the rich and famous and powerful, all of that attention appears to compensate them for all the drawbacks of getting to where they are and staying there. Smith continues, writing of the relentless attention that the famous receive:

> It is this, which, notwithstanding the restraint it imposes, notwithstanding the loss of liberty with which it is attended, renders greatness the object of envy, and compensates, in the opinion of mankind, all that toil, all that anxiety, all those mortifications which must be undergone in the pursuit of it; and what is of yet more consequence, all that leisure, all that ease, all that careless security, which are forfeited for ever by the acquisition.

What Smith is saying in this passage is that if you want to be rich and famous, powerful and successful, you have to give up leisure and ease and careless security forever. And you have to toil and have anxiety and endure "mortifications"—pain and shame—if you want to make it. You have to work hard. You have to give up tranquillity. In return you get a great deal of attention. People want to know what you think, they look to you for how to dress and speak and behave. When you enter a room, all eyes are on you. And the envy and admiration that everyone else has for the great makes the price that is paid worthwhile, at least in the eyes of many.

When I would talk with my students about this passage of Smith's, I'd ask them to imagine what would happen to our class if two major-league celebrities, say Angelina Jolie and Brad Pitt, wandered into our classroom in search of a better understanding of *The Theory of Moral Sentiments.* Imagine them quietly entering the room at the start of class and sitting off to the side, attentive, interested, ready to take notes if anything catches their fancy. What would happen to the class? Would any of the students be able to pay me the slightest attention? All eyes would be on Brangelina. And I'd probably be staring at them too. It's hard to act normally in the presence of an extremely famous person. Even famous people can be made to feel like children in the presence of other famous people.

We think so highly of rich and famous people that we imagine, says Smith, that their lives are nearly perfect. We idealize their lives to such a degree that we find their deaths to be unusually painful. Why? It's like a perfect symphony marred by a discordant note at the very end.

> What pity, we think, that any thing should spoil and corrupt so agreeable a situation! We could even wish them immortal; and it seems hard to us, that death should at last put an end to such perfect enjoyment. It is cruel, we think, in Nature to compel them from their exalted sta-

tions to that humble, but hospitable home, which she has provided for all her children.

Rather than merely envying the rich and famous, Smith is saying that we imagine they deserve a fate better than the rest of us. Somehow, they should be able to cheat death. When death comes, it's like a fairy tale with a dark ending instead of the perfect conclusion we long for. I don't know if Smith is right about the cause, but it's certainly true that we mourn the death of celebrities with surprising intensity. Princess Di, Elvis Presley, Whitney Houston—their deaths produced an outpouring of grief seemingly out of line with what was lost. And, as Smith observed, the outpouring of grief often dwarfs the way we respond to the deaths and tragedies of everyday people.

> Every calamity that befals them, every injury that is done them, excites in the breast of the spectator ten times more compassion and resentment than he would have felt, had the same things happened to other men.

Smith notes that we have a particular romance for the politically powerful. In his day, kings and lords were the politically great. In our day, we have dictators who appear to be revered. But even democratic leaders have enough power to get their share of adulation, a share that to Smith and me seems out of line with their actual accomplishments. The assassination of a king—or a president—seems so much worse than the murder of an everyday person:

> The traitor who conspires against the life of his monarch, is thought a greater monster than any other murderer. All the innocent blood that was shed in the civil wars, provoked less indignation than the death of Charles I.

Smith continues by arguing that to watch how people respond to the deaths of the great and famous and powerful compared with normal human beings, you'd think that pain and death must feel different to the great compared with everyone else:

> A stranger to human nature, who saw the indifference of men about the misery of their inferiors, and the regret and indignation which they feel for the misfortunes and sufferings of those above them, would be apt to imagine, that pain must be more agonizing, and the convulsions of death more terrible to persons of higher rank, than to those of meaner stations.

Because of our romantic views of their happiness and importance, we are happy, in Smith's eyes, to be subservient to the politically powerful and even to tolerate their abuse. Even the tyrant can be adored because of our inclination to be overly sympathetic to greatness. To oppose the tyrant goes against our nature, not because it is dangerous, says Smith, but because we idealize his greatness and happiness.

> Even when the order of society seems to require that we should oppose them, we can hardly bring ourselves to do it.

Think of Chavez or Castro or even the way many Russian people today romanticize Stalin. People have an admiration for these monsters that is difficult to explain. Logic may decree that a king deserves to be overthrown, but our hearts find it difficult.

> That kings are the servants of the people, to be obeyed, resisted, deposed, or punished, as the public conveniency may require, is the doctrine of reason and philosophy; but it is not the doctrine of Nature.

We stand in awe of the powerful. We seek their favor even if it is nothing more than a pleasant glance in return for serving them:

> Nature would teach us to submit to them for their own sake, to tremble and bow down before their exalted sta-

tion, to regard their smile as a reward sufficient to compensate any services, and to dread their displeasure, though no other evil were to follow from it, as the severest of all mortifications.

Smith goes on to say that it is nearly impossible to treat kings as we would treat anyone else unless they are longtime acquaintances:

To treat them in any respect as men, to reason and dispute with them upon ordinary occasions, requires such resolution, that there are few men whose magnanimity can support them in it, unless they are likewise assisted by familiarity and acquaintance.

I've met a few exceedingly wealthy men and women, seen senators up close. I've met a few rock stars and shaken hands with Muhammad Ali and Prince Charles. Such people almost seem to be a different species. The adoration they receive makes them glow with a light that is different from what you and I give off. When James Cameron won the Oscar for best director for *Titanic* and crowed, "I'm king of the world," he wasn't just quoting from the screenplay. He dropped the mask and gave us a glimpse of his true self. He was telling the audience that he was worthy of attention, supreme attention. Look at me, he seemed to be saying. Pay me homage. I'm at the top.

It must be a terrible drug, the drug of celebrity. Once you have been famous, once you have been not just respected by the masses but adored, the normal pleasures of life no longer satisfy:

> To those who have been accustomed to the possession, or even to the hope of public admiration, all other pleasures sicken and decay. Of all the discarded statesmen who for their own ease have studied to get the better of ambition, and to despise those honours which they could no longer arrive at, how few have been able to succeed?

Think of the aging rock star, still touring, still seeking the adulation of the crowd even though the crowd is getting smaller with each passing year. Think of the aging athlete, past his prime, still playing. When Marilyn Monroe returned from entertaining troops in Korea, she told her husband, "Joe, you never heard such cheering!" Of course, it was just a figure of speech meaning there was a lot of cheering. But her husband, Joe DiMaggio, one of the greatest baseball players of all time, answered quietly, "Yes, I have." What is it like, to take the field day after day to wild cheering? For so many, it must be a drug whose dose must be increased to achieve the same thrill. Is achieving fame and success a blessing or a curse?

I have a friend whose son is a Hollywood actor. By the standards of the profession he is an incredible success—he has had two or three speaking roles in major Hollywood films. But they were small roles, just a few lines. Still, that puts him in a very select group of people relative to the number who want to be in the movies. But you've never heard of him. He's done some TV, but he's not a star. I'm sure he is disappointed not to be more successful. I'm sure he aspired to stardom. I've often wondered whether his parents share his disappointment. Did they want him to have Brad Pitt's life? Would you want that for yourself or your son? Are movie stars happy? Can they have anything like a normal life? Can they have a normal marriage? And yet, like football coaches, the line is long for those who want the job.

You might think you'd be thrilled to have Brad Pitt's life. What could be better? A beautiful wife. Incredible wealth. Unbelievable fame. And yet so many wildly successful people in the public eye don't seem particularly happy. Look at Elvis Presley, Whitney Houston, Michael Jackson, or Marilyn Monroe. The thrill was gone, and no thrill could make up for what was lost. The satisfaction of past accomplishments did not console.

You'd think being the greatest golfer of all time, or maybe second-greatest on the way to being the greatest, having a Swedish model for a wife, and, on top of that, having $600 million would lead to some contentment and happiness. That life was evidently insufficiently satisfying for Tiger Woods. He ended up being chased by his wife as she swung a golf club at him. We're just not wired to be content with what we have, no matter how much.

For Smith, ambition—the desire to be rich or famous or both—is a poison to be avoided. Once you get on that treadmill, there is no rest.

Are you in earnest resolved never to barter your liberty for the lordly servitude of a court, but to live free, fearless, and independent? There seems to be one way to continue in that virtuous resolution; and perhaps but one. Never enter the place from whence so few have been able to return; never come within the circle of ambition; nor ever bring yourself into comparison with those masters of the earth who have already engrossed the attention of half mankind before you.

How do you reconcile these views with Smith's own share of fame and riches? If I could quiz him in front of that warm fire, his good scotch in my hand, I think he'd answer the way he would about money. It's not unpleasant. It just shouldn't be pursued for its own sake. Stay humble, my friend, he'd say. If you can, do what you love, do what you respect, and be content if that feeds your family. Everything beyond that is gravy.

As I write these words, a Saudi prince is suing Forbes for ranking him as the twenty-sixth richest person in the world. He felt they'd underestimated his wealth. He wanted to be ranked higher. Doesn't Prince Alwaleed bin Talal have something better to do? He might try wagging more and barking less.

There will always be someone richer than you, more skilled than you, more famous than you. Who is rich? asks the Talmud. He who is happy with his lot. Maybe it is easier to be happy with what you have if you know that inside you is the urge for attention that Smith identifies.

Smith is showing us a better path to contentment than the one the world holds out to seduce us with. There is another way to be loved. Instead of pursuing attention via wealth or fame or power, pursue wisdom and goodness. There are two ways to be loved, to satisfy the desire we all have in us to be noticed and to be somebody. The first path is to be rich, famous, powerful. The second path is to be wise and virtuous.

Two different models, two different pictures, are held out to us, according to which we may fashion our own character and behaviour; the one more gaudy and glittering in its colouring; the other more correct and more exquisitely beautiful in its outline: the one forcing itself upon the notice of every wandering eye; the other, attracting the attention of scarce any body but the most studious and careful observer.

The road paved with wealth, fame, and power is the gaudier road, the glittering road, the one that draws us. Yet the other road is the better road. Less gaudy, generally glitter-free, but still exquisitely beautiful. On one road, the traveler is noticed by everyone. If you take the other road, the road of wisdom and virtue, you will also be loved. You will also be respected. You will also be noticed. But only by the "most studious and careful observer." The cheering will be much quieter and the crowd much smaller.

Smith, in his personal life, tried to be worthy of respect and admiration. He was a good friend, a good son, a good teacher. He gained wisdom. He acted with virtue. And as a result he was loved. Not just by the studious and careful observer, but by the world down through the ages. But I'd like to think that his immortality wasn't what he planned or sought. It was gravy. It came to him, but he never sought it out. He took the quiet road, the one less traveled.

We can get a glimpse of what that road may have been like for Smith from a story his biographer, John Rae, tells about a dinner party Smith enjoyed in London in 1787 at the house of Henry Dundas in Wimbledon Green. The illustrious guests that night included the prime minister, William Pitt, whom Rae describes as one of Smith's "most convinced disciples" and who at the time was "reforming the national finances with the *Wealth of Nations* in his hand." Smith was no fan of politicians or kings, but he did have some respect for what Smith called a statesman, and Pitt, Smith is reported to have said, understood Smith's work better than he did. Two future prime ministers—William Grenville and Henry Addington—were also there, along with a fervent abolitionist, William Wilberforce, whose cause Smith supported. Smith was one of the last guests to arrive, and the company all stood to greet him and remained standing. Smith urged them to sit down, but Pitt reportedly replied, "No, we will stand till you are first seated, for we are all your scholars." That sign of respect for Smith's loveliness—a loveliness born of wisdom and virtue rather than fame, power, or wealth—must have pleased Smith.

Smith in his book and with his life is telling us how to live. Seek wisdom and virtue. Behave as if an impartial spectator is watching you. Use the idea of an impartial spectator to step outside yourself and see yourself as others see you. Use that vision to know yourself. Avoid the seductions of money and fame, for they will never satisfy.

How to be virtuous is not so obvious, and that comes next. But I want to close this chapter with Peter Buffett, the man who ended up selling his Berkshire Hathaway stock for $90,000 and giving up the $100 million he could have had in order to pursue a career as a musician.

A few years ago, Peter Buffett reflected on his decision to sell his Berkshire Hathaway stock to pursue his dreams in his memoir, *Life Is What You Make It*. He claims to have no regrets. But could a life as a successful musician possibly be worth giving up $100 million? Wouldn't $100 million be even more pleasant?

Then you ask yourself—what could he have with the extra millions? A nicer car? He could have a Lamborghini Veneno Roadster that retails for about $4 million. Or he could settle for the lovely Ferrari Spider, at $300,000; he could have a couple of those. He could have a mansion you and I can only imagine, anywhere in the world. Like Onassis, he could own an island or two rather than enduring the indignity of visiting an island in the Mediterranean, say, and having to share it with others while staying at a nice hotel. Could those physical pleasures possibly be worth sacrificing the life in music that he dreamed of and ultimately achieved? I think Peter Buffett got a bargain. He gave up $100 million and got something—hard as it is to imagine—that was even more precious. A good life. I think Adam Smith would agree with me.

Chapter 6

How to Be Lovely

Smith's prescription for happiness is a simple formula. To be content, you need to be loved and to be lovely. You need to be respected and respectable. You need to be praised and praiseworthy. You need to matter to other people, and you need for their image of you to be the real you–you need to earn their respect and honor and admiration honestly.

There are two ways to be loved. You can be rich and famous. Or you can be wise and virtuous. Choose the second way, Smith counsels, the way of wisdom and virtue. Be lovely. So if you want to be happy, be lovely. But what is loveliness? What is virtue? Not so simple. Smith has two answers for how to be lovely—how to be respected, admired, and worthy of praise. The first is a minimum standard, what Smith calls propriety.

Propriety is an old-fashioned word. The modern version is *proper* or *appropriate*. *Proper behavior* sounds stuffy, like something out of finishing school. But all Smith means by propriety or proper behavior is an idea we all understand— acting appropriately. And by appropriately, he means meeting the expectations of those around us—acting in the way that they expect and that allows them to interact with us in the way that we expect.

While I was in my early twenties, I spent a summer in Santiago, Chile, doing economics research. Toward the end of my stay, I spent a week house-sitting for an older colleague. Coming home from work the first night, I let myself in, sat on the couch, put my feet up, and started reading the newspaper, enjoying the spacious surroundings, which were a step up from my small apartment. To my utter surprise, a woman emerged from the kitchen. My colleague had neglected to tell me that his house came with a house-keeper.

She smiled and asked me something. My Spanish was very mediocre; she spoke no English. But it was clear that she wanted to know what I wanted for dinner. A stranger making dinner for me already made me uncomfortable. I certainly wasn't going to tell her what to make. So I said whatever she wanted to make was fine. Now it was her turn to be uncomfortable. That mystified me just as much as my response had confused her. Giving her the option to make whatever she wanted was my way of trying to be nice. Instead, I had put her in a situation she wasn't accustomed to and didn't expect. I had acted improperly.

We somehow worked out what she was going to make for dinner, and she went into the kitchen while I returned to the couch. It seemed weird that this woman I didn't know and who didn't work for me was making me dinner while I relaxed in the living room. I committed another faux pas, another violation of propriety—I went into the kitchen to keep her company. That seemed thoughtful, but again I failed to reckon with her expectations. When I opened the door, she was totally taken aback to find me in her territory. She blushed. Was something wrong? she asked. No, I reassured her, and another awkward silence prevailed. I realized that I had broken some social convention, but once I was in the kitchen, talking seemed in order, so I did the best I could.

The talking didn't go well either. I figured music was a safe topic. What kind of music did she like? Julio Iglesias and Frank Sinatra. At the time, I didn't enjoy listening to either one, though I at least had the presence of mind to keep my views to myself. (I later became a big Sinatra fan.) I tried desperately to think of something else to say. Sports! What about soccer? Was she a *fútbol* fan? She was. What was her favorite team? Cola Cola, she said. She asked me for my favorite team. Universidad de Chile, I replied. My friends from the research institute where I worked, budding economists, all followed Universidad de Chile, so I did too. Later I discovered that Cola Cola was the team that the poor people of Santiago all rooted for; Universidad de Chile was the team for college graduates.

In my urge to reduce the distance between us, I had reminded her of our social differences. Ignorant and unaware, I had violated one social convention after another. The problem wasn't my goal of interacting with this woman. The problem was that I didn't know the proper way to do it. My intentions were honorable. My behavior was not dishonorable; but it was not proper. As a result, I made her very uncomfortable. But it was worse than that—by failing to meet the expectations and plans of the housekeeper, I had made her job more difficult. Propriety goes a long way toward making life a little easier than it otherwise would be.

In the twenty-first century we have an almost iconic respect for certain kinds of *impropriety*. Get on YouTube and listen to Steve Jobs read the text of his "Think Different" ad—"Here's to the crazy ones." It's an homage to breaking the rules. Or consider Jobs himself, a contrarian in both his personal and professional life in so many ways. We live in an ironic age, an age when contrary behavior, spontaneous behavior, behavior that is outside the box, seems often to be viewed with more esteem than proper behavior. Think of Muhammad Ali, Madonna, and Bob Dylan. All three made immense amounts of money augmenting their skills with behavior that flouted convention. But they and those like them are the exceptions. For every Howard Stern, there are many more like Oprah Winfrey. For every Allen Iverson, there are many more like Michael Jordan.

Most of us, in our daily lives, encourage proper and appropriate behavior. Telling our children that some behavior or other is inappropriate is the modern mantra of parental disapproval. And we raise our kids that way because we understand how important it is to meet the expectations of the people around us. We teach our children to say "please" and "thank you." We teach them the difference between an indoor voice and an outdoor voice. We teach them to eat somewhat graciously. The propriety of chewing with your mouth closed is timeless.

As adults, we have a similar set of rules about what is

proper that we rarely think about consciously. When a friend comes back from vacation, you ask her about her trip. When a friend has a worried look on his face, you ask him if anything is wrong. When a stranger on the subway has a worried look, you don't say anything. But if a stranger looks lost and disoriented, it's OK to offer to help. When you're in Rome, do as the Romans do. When you're in Santiago, learn the expectations of your housekeeper and try to meet them.

We live in rings of intimacy. We don't treat those closest to us the same way we treat people who are further away. And among those who are closest to us, there are expectations of reciprocity and sometimes no expectations at all. Flowers for my wife on a random Tuesday are sometimes better than flowers on her birthday.

Meeting expectations of what is proper allows those around us to interact with us effectively and, more than that, with grace and style and pleasure. Propriety is about playing your part in the human symphony. There can be solos and improvisation, but these novelties work best when they take place in expected ways.

Our age is less formal than Smith's. In 2014, it's proper for a waiter to introduce himself to you by his first name. A man can campaign for the leadership of his country wearing jeans. A woman can ask a man out on a date and pursue him aggressively. None of these things were proper in 1759. It's proper today to walk around with a weird object sticking out of your ear, murmuring into the ether. In 1759, that was a sign of social dysfunction, perhaps madness. Today it means you're talking on your cell phone. But despite these differences, what hasn't changed is that some things are appropriate in various social settings, and some things are inappropriate.

Smith's discussion of propriety is less about fashion and etiquette and more about our emotions and our reactions to the emotions of others—our ability to be sympathetic or unsympathetic to the emotions and experiences of those around us. His book, after all, is about our moral sentiments. Smith focuses on how we approve or disapprove of other people's behavior depending on whether their reactions match ours. So if you roar at a joke that I also find hilarious, I approve of your laughter. If you cry at a tragedy that also breaks my heart, I approve. You're crazy about that new pop song and I can't get it out of my head either—that's perfect. But in other cases, our reactions may not match:

> If my animosity goes beyond what the indignation of my friend can correspond to; if my grief exceeds what his most tender compassion can go along with; if my admiration is either too high or too low to tally with his own;

if I laugh loud and heartily when he only smiles, or, on the contrary, only smile when he laughs loud and heartily; . . .

In those cases, when our responses are so out of sync, says Smith, we disapprove. Propriety is about matching our responses to those around us.

This seems rather harsh. Are we that judgmental? If the death of my cat leaves me sobbing and cats leave you cold, will you really disapprove of my reaction? If I laud George Jones's classic "He Stopped Loving Her Today" as one of the greatest songs of all time because it almost always brings me near to tears, but you find it trite and predictable, shouldn't we both just shrug and say there's no disputing tastes? You like the Three Stooges; I prefer the Marx Brothers. You like Charlie Chaplin; I like Buster Keaton. You like *Dumb & Dumber*, and I like *Groundhog Day*. What's the big deal? Live and let live. Do we really disapprove of the reactions of others and base our disapproval on our own reactions?

The social pressure to be tolerant of other people's behavior and certainly their choices seems to disprove Smith's claim. Tolerance is the great religion of modern times; we all bow to it in ways that Smith would have found surprising. Yet despite the pressure to live and let live, our inner emotions often mirror the examples Smith provides. His insights help explain the strange phenomenon of people trying to convince others to like the same movie or song that they do. Excessive grief or inadequate grief embarrasses us and makes us uncomfortable. When a political scandal is in the news and our friends take a different perspective, it makes us uneasy and sometimes angry.

And the greater the gap between my sentiments and yours, the more you and I will disapprove of each other's reactions, seeing them as improper. We prefer harmony in our mutual sentiments to disharmony. This idea of harmony—of the matching of my reactions to yours, and vice versa—runs through Smith's discussion of emotions and social interactions.

The gap between my sentiments and yours is much more consequential, says Smith, when it's a personal example, as opposed to your feelings about a poem, a song, or a work of art. It's much more important to me that you like my friends than my favorite poems. I want you to like my friends and dislike my enemies. But I can live with the fact that you don't like my friends as much as I do or even that you don't befriend them at all. I care more, says Smith, that you dislike my enemies.

But what we care most strongly about is not harmony of taste about art, or harmony of taste about our friends and enemies. What I really want, says Smith, is that your emotions harmonize with my own as I face tragedy or triumph. If I am trying to cope with a tragedy, I want you to enter into my grief. Smith argues that if you share some of my grief, I will be consoled; by empathizing with my situation in harmony with my own response, something extraordinary happens—you take some of my grief away.

You can only imagine my grief; you cannot match it. You can't put yourself in my emotional shoes. You aren't me. You can only imagine what it would be like to go through what I'm going through. Your own situation, your own problems, your own fears, even your own pleasures, intrude. So we do the best we can.

Sticking with the musical metaphor, if my singing voice is louder than yours, our duet won't sound very nice. I drown you out, and your singing fails to enhance mine. Because I know you can't feel my pain the way I feel it, I soften my grief in your presence. Rather than expecting you to sing as loudly as I do, I lower my voice instead. You, in turn, try to sing a little louder. I calibrate my emotional response to what I think is your potential level of sympathy. This explains why I can cry more easily in front of my family than in front of friends. And I can cry more comfortably around friends than in front of strangers.

Emotional interaction is a duet in which we are constantly fine-tuning our volume to match that of our fellow. When I am suffering, you imagine being in my situation and feel some of my sadness. I see you striving to match my grief. But, Smith notes, this can't be done as perfectly with emotions as it can be done in song. We're human. If I suffer a tragedy, there is a limit to how much you can feel my pain and a limit to how much I can temper my reaction. But the closer the intensity of our reactions, the more comfort I will feel. That encourages me to lower the intensity of my response and for you to increase yours:

> To see the emotions of their hearts, in every respect, beat time to his own, in the violent and disagreeable passions, constitutes his sole consolation. But he can only hope to obtain this by lowering his passion to that pitch, in which the spectators are capable of going along with him.

To capture this idea of the mutual matching of emotional intensity, Smith uses a musical metaphor—the flattening of the sharpness of a musical note to create harmony. He asks the reader's permission to use the metaphor:

> He must flatten, if I may be allowed to say so, the sharpness of its natural tone, in order to reduce it to harmony and concord with the emotions of those who are about him.

Thus the sufferer strives to dampen his passion. The bystanders, through compassion, try to feel the pain of the sufferer and cannot. The experiences are simply not the same:

> What they feel, will, indeed, always be, in some respects, different from what he feels, and compassion can never be exactly the same with original sorrow; because the secret consciousness that the change of situations, from which the sympathetic sentiment arises, is but imaginary, not only lowers it in degree, but, in some measure, varies it in kind, and gives it a quite different modification.

But a match isn't necessary for the sufferer to be comforted. Smith again uses a musical metaphor:

> These two sentiments, however, may, it is evident, have such a correspondence with one another, as is sufficient for the harmony of society. Though they will never be unisons, they may be concords, and this is all that is wanted or required.

In music, a unison occurs when two notes are exactly the same. If they are different yet still sound good together, the notes are said to be concordant. Concordance is the best we can hope for. The result is harmony, in which the sufferer is consoled and the consolers have reduced the sufferer's suffering.

Smith's analysis of the music of suffering explains why our grief around strangers or even acquaintances and some friends is so tempered. If you don't know me well or if you don't know me at all, your ability to feel my pain is much weaker than if we are friends or family. So I bring the level of my grief way down, knowing that your ability to empathize with me is so limited.

In Smith's view, my friend's company can dissipate my grief:

> The mind, therefore, is rarely so disturbed, but that the company of a friend will restore it to some degree of tranquillity and sedateness. The breast is, in some measure, calmed and composed the moment we come into his presence.

How this happens is rather extraordinary:

> We are immediately put in mind of the light in which he will view our situation, and we begin to view it ourselves in the same light; for the effect of sympathy is instantaneous.

Part of the comfort we receive from a friend comes from experiencing our pain through the friend's eyes. Because the friend is less pained than we can be, we are less pained. We watch our friend watching us, and seeing ourselves through our friend's eyes lessens the tragedy. That's a friend; at the next level is an acquaintance, and then finally a stranger. As we move further and further away from a friend or loved one, we realize that those around us have only modest sympathy for our situation:

> We expect less sympathy from a common acquaintance than from a friend: we cannot open to the former all those little circumstances which we can unfold to the latter: we assume, therefore, more tranquillity before him, and endeavour to fix our thoughts upon those general outlines of our situation which he is willing to consider. We expect still less sympathy from an assembly of strangers, and we assume, therefore, still more tranquillity before them, and always endeavour to bring down our passion to that pitch, which the particular company we are in may be expected to go along with.

Smith then makes the rather extraordinary claim that because strangers feel our pain less intensely than an acquaintance who in turn feels our pain less intensely than a friend or loved one, being around strangers helps us regain our emotional equilibrium even more effectively than being with a friend.

> Nor is this only an assumed appearance: for if we are at all masters of ourselves, the presence of a mere acquaintance will really compose us, still more than that of a friend; and that of an assembly of strangers still more than that of an acquaintance.

In other words, after some emotional challenge, when we pull ourselves together in front of a group of strangers we're not just putting up a brave front. We actually feel better. The relative calm of the stranger, transmitted to us because of the stranger's inability to fully sympathize with our situation, actually has a beneficial effect.

You can see this effect in action in modern life if you're having an argument with a family member. The argument starts to get heated and you can feel yourself starting to get really angry. The other person gets more heated as well. Then your cell phone rings. You look at the caller ID. It's a co-worker with a tight deadline whom you promised to help. When you say hello, your voice is normal. All the anger you had from the argument disappears. How is that possible? It's not conscious, but the phone call from the relative stranger turns your anger off. You weren't faking the anger before. And you're not faking being calm once you answer the phone. You've actually calmed down.

My great-great-grandmother, who must have been born around 1870, told my father that if he was ever down or depressed he should go outside and tell his troubles to a rock. Abraham Lincoln used to write angry letters of recrimination to his generals and put them away, unsent, in a drawer. Sometimes it's good to get something out of your system without anyone other than yourself knowing about it. One of the best pieces of advice I've ever received is to hold your anger for a day before you think of acting on it. The mere passage of time softens the emotion and can prevent you from saying or doing something stupid—or, worse, destructive—that you will inevitably regret.

Smith's claims about our emotions create another way to understand these ideas. Talking to a rock or writing a letter to someone who will never see it is a way of tapping into Smith's insight about strangers. What is less empathetic than a rock? Or the file drawer that receives the unsent letter? Or, in modern times, when you send an e-mail into the "Drafts" folder? Maybe the value of these exercises isn't just the expression of the emotion but the expressing of it to someone or some *thing* that isn't empathetic at all.

Just as it is proper to express our anger or grief differently across the spectrum of intimacy from stranger to close friend, we do the same thing with joy. You get a promotion or a raise or a great evaluation, or your proposal is accepted. You can't wait to get home and tell your husband. As you get off the subway, you run into a neighbor, a friend you see from time to time at school events. You enjoy talking to her, sharing the latest events in your lives. She asks what's going on. You want to burst into song. My proposal was accepted! I won the competition! But you don't. That would be an example of impropriety. You don't know your neighbor well enough. Instead, you try to calm the exuberance showing on your face. You keep your song to yourself. You just smile and say, things are good, how are you doing? But when you see your husband, the good news bursts out of you and you embrace each other, beaming with the joy of it. You share the biggest successes and happinesses in your life with your spouse, your parents, and your closest friends. And even your closest friends may have trouble feeling your joy in the same way that you do.

Smith notes a number of differences between how we react to grief and joy that is felt by others:

There is, however, this difference between grief and joy, that we are generally most disposed to sympathize with small joys and great sorrows.

So I am happy when you have some success. But if you have great and sudden success, I may have trouble being happy for you. Envy can raise its ugly head.

The man who, by some sudden revolution of fortune, is lifted up all at once into a condition of life, greatly above what he had formerly lived in, may be assured that the congratulations of his best friends are not all of them perfectly sincere.

The writer Gore Vidal said it a little more bluntly, "Every time a friend succeeds, I die a little." Smith suggests that the man who has had some large and sudden success will realize that envy makes it difficult for others to share in his joy. The successful man will mute his trumpeting of his good fortune. He will affect humility, probably unsuccessfully. But he will at least try.

Little day-to-day joys, says Smith—good humor and people in good spirits generally—bring out in us a good mood and a general feeling of happiness. So we share those easily with our friends and acquaintances, and they in turn bounce good feelings back to us. We share our big successes only with our best friends and family.

But with grief the ease of sharing is in the other direction. We can share tragedies with strangers more easily than what Smith calls "small vexations." We don't sympathize with someone who is annoyed by those small vexations. Smith makes a fabulous list of the whiner's catalog of grievances, the man who complains about his cook's performance, the impoliteness of a colleague, travel woes, inadequate sunshine on a visit to the country, and my favorite, the family member who fails to pay complete attention when being told a story:

> The man who is made uneasy by every little disagreeable incident, who is hurt if either the cook or the butler have failed in the least article of their duty, who feels every defect in the highest ceremonial of politeness, whether it be shewn to himself or to any other person, who takes it amiss that his intimate friend did not bid him good-morrow when they met in the forenoon, and that his brother hummed a tune all the time he himself was telling a story; who is put out of humour by the badness of the weather when in the country, by the badness of the roads when upon a journey, and by the want of company, and dulness of all public diversions when in town; such

a person, I say, though he should have some reason, will seldom meet with much sympathy.

And it's a little worse than that, says Smith. Not only do we have trouble sympathizing with those small vexations—what we might call inconveniences—but we are likely to see them as humorous and entertaining.

There is, besides, a malice in mankind, which not only prevents all sympathy with little uneasinesses, but renders them in some measure diverting.

Because of our lack of sympathy, Smith says it's common for people to hide their vexation or annoyance at small inconveniences or even to make fun of themselves over what they've endured. We don't look for sympathy in those situations. We make light of what we've experienced, beating our friends to the punch and showing that such "uneasinesses" are no big deal to us. We're made of sterner stuff. Some of my favorite stories are the ones my brother tells me about his travel troubles. He doesn't complain about them. He turns them into comedy routines.

But what Smith calls the "deep distress" of our neighbor brings out strong and sincere sympathy. To make his point, Smith notes that we can weep over a book or play (or movie) even though we know the tragedy is fictional. A great work of art (and sometimes even a cheesy one) can tap into the natural sympathy we have for true tragedy. Real tragedy brings out an even stronger response, especially when it visits our loved ones. Sharing grief yields sympathy and comfort. But if you're jilted by your mistress, says Smith, laugh it off. Give your friends a little diversion with the story of your modest misfortune.

Smith's example of how to deal with a friend jilted by his mistress highlights just how different propriety is at different times and in different cultures. Smith would find our informal culture bewildering. But I can't imagine a buddy publicly complaining about being jilted by his mistress. We live in tolerant times, but at least in the circles in which I travel, mistresses, rebellious or otherwise, don't make for water-cooler conversation.

While the first asymmetry Smith identifies is that we find it easier to sympathize with small joys and great sorrows, our emotional response to joy and sorrow is also unequal. Smith says we generally sympathize more with joy than with grief. Our joy at a wedding is much greater than our sorrow at a funeral. At a funeral, our sorrow "amounts to no more than an affected gravity," says Smith. But at a wedding we are genuinely joyous for the participants. We

are even, says Smith, as happy as they are, at least for the
moment:

> Whenever we cordially congratulate our friends, which,
> however, to the disgrace of human nature, we do but sel-
> dom, their joy literally becomes our joy: we are, for the
> moment, as happy as they are: our heart swells and over-
> flows with real pleasure: joy and complacency sparkle
> from our eyes, and animate every feature of our counte-
> nance, and every gesture of our body.

However, when we offer our condolences to our friends,
we cannot match their emotions:

> But, on the contrary, when we condole with our friends
> in their afflictions, how little do we feel, in comparison
> of what they feel? We sit down by them, we look at them,
> and while they relate to us the circumstances of their
> misfortune, we listen to them with gravity and atten-
> tion.

When a friend has a broken heart, we cannot match the
feeling. Smith says we feel bad that we can't sympathize
effectively, and so we try to artificially create a feeling of
sympathy. Even if we succeed, the feeling disappears
quickly.

But while their narration is every moment interrupted by those natural bursts of passion which often seem almost to choak them in the midst of it; how far are the languid emotions of our hearts from keeping time to the transports of theirs? We may be sensible, at the same time, that their passion is natural, and no greater than what we ourselves might feel upon the like occasion. We may even inwardly reproach ourselves with our own want of sensibility, and perhaps, on that account, work ourselves up into an artificial sympathy, which, however, when it is raised, is always the slightest and most transitory imaginable; and generally, as soon as we have left the room, vanishes, and is gone for ever.

Despite the transitory nature of our sympathy with the suffering of others, Smith concludes that we have just the right amount of concern for others. If we had more, we would find life difficult to bear. Less, and we would be unable to comfort our friends in hard times:

Nature, it seems, when she loaded us with our own sorrows, thought that they were enough, and therefore did not command us to take any further share in those of others, than what was necessary to prompt us to relieve them.

We have enough troubles of our own. Taking on the suffering of others in full measure would be too hard. Our ability to sympathize with others is limited. But that limited amount is enough to bring them consolation.

A few days before I wrote this chapter, a good friend told me that a beloved cousin of his was dying. They were very close, and the cousin was one of the last members of that generation whom he knew well. I could tell how sad my friend was, and I sympathized with his sadness. I'm sure my face was solemn. I put my hand on his shoulder and told him how bad I felt for him. I asked him to keep me posted on his cousin's health. I was truly sad for my friend. I felt some of his pain, but not enough to bring down my spirits for more than the briefest time. I was sad for him, but not actually sad. Just as Smith suggests, I quickly forgot about my friend's sadness and distress other than to mention it to my wife. A few weeks earlier, the same friend had had a great success that he shared with me. I was happy for him. In that case, his success actually put me in a good mood. I wasn't just happy for him. I was happy, period.

This asymmetry of joy and sorrow—the ease with which we sympathize with success relative to failure—is Smith's explanation for why the rich and famous receive more attention and create more happiness than the poor and forgotten. We enjoy the successes of the rich and famous. The poor and forgotten move us briefly and not deeply. For Smith, this explains why rich people flaunt their wealth and poor people hide what they are missing:

> It is because mankind are disposed to sympathize more entirely with our joy than with our sorrow, that we make parade of our riches, and conceal our poverty. Nothing is so mortifying as to be obliged to expose our distress to the view of the public, and to feel, that though our situation is open to the eyes of all mankind, no mortal conceives for us the half of what we suffer. Nay, it is chiefly from this regard to the sentiments of mankind, that we pursue riches and avoid poverty.

Smith's observations on how we interact with others in grief and in joy are mainly about how we are made—the nature of human nature—and not so much about how we should behave. He is saying that there are fundamental differences in how we can sympathize with those around us. There are limits to sympathy as we go from experiencing the emotions of close friends compared with those of strangers. We don't experience great grief the same way we experience great joy. The joy of others can make us happy, as long as we are not envious. The grief of others has a much more limited effect, even for close friends.

How do these lessons translate into propriety? We all differ in how well we process social signals. Some people do it effortlessly, others struggle. To return to Smith's musical metaphor, some people have perfect pitch, while others are tone-deaf. When we have some great success, do we share it with someone who cannot enjoy it because it reminds them of some success they missed? They won't be able to enjoy your success. It will bring them pain. When someone is in pain, do you overcome your natural indifference to show them that you are hearing their sadness? When you're in pain, do you share too much emotion with someone who simply can't handle it?

Smith is telling us what others can handle, what others can share and what is appropriate to share, what is appropriate to say in response to those around us. He is sensitizing us to our own imperfection and what we might do to overcome the shortcomings in our emotional interactions. Few of us have perfect pitch. Smith is helping us find the right tone to strike when we listen to our friends and when they listen to us. He is telling us what is proper in our emotional interactions with close friends, casual acquaintances, and strangers.

Behaving with propriety is the ability to conform to the expectations of those around us, and they in turn conform to our expectations. When we conform to such expectations, we allow those around us to trust us. That trust allows us to share our emotions with each other at the right level of intensity for the different rings of intimacy we inhabit. That's the beginning of loveliness, of earning the respect of those around us, along with self-respect.

Acting with propriety is one measure of what Smith would call a gentleman. Propriety—that is, acting properly—gains you the approval of those around you, says Smith. But it is not admired or celebrated. For admiration and celebration, you need virtue.

Chapter 7

How to Be Good

Smith encourages us to be virtuous as the better way to being loved. But what exactly does Smith mean by virtue? Virtue is multifaceted for Smith, but his big three are prudence, justice, and beneficence. These are the traits that make us lovely and that in turn make us respected and admired by those around us—the traits that make us loved.

What does Smith mean by prudence, justice, and beneficence? For Smith, prudence means, in modern terms, taking care of yourself, justice means not hurting others, and beneficence means being good to others. That's not a bad trio for thinking about how to live the good life. Be good to yourself and be good to others. You do good to others by not hurting them and by helping them when you can.

To be prudent, in modern English, means to not act recklessly. But Smith means much more than that. He means taking care of yourself in the full sense of the phrase "taking care." For Smith, prudence covers everything in your personal bearing, the "wise and judicious care" of your health, your money, and your reputation. So the modern prudent man doesn't smoke. He's physically active and keeps his weight under control. He works hard and avoids debt. He stays away from get-rich-quick schemes. I would suggest that he prefers indexed mutual funds to managed funds and stock picking. In short, he foregoes the potential of a large upside to avoid the downside.

But how does the prudent man take care of his reputation? Smith's advice is timeless but a bit of a challenge for modern sensibilities.

The prudent man, says Smith, is sincere and honest. At the same time, he doesn't volunteer everything he knows; he is reserved and cautious in his speech and his action. He doesn't stick his opinion into every discussion. He's a good friend, but he manages to avoid melodrama in his relationships. His friendships are a "faithful attachment to a few well-tried and well-chosen companions"; he chooses his friends not because they're cool or have an impressive list of accomplishments, but because they have the "sober esteem of modesty, discretion, and good conduct."

The prudent man is not a party animal: "He rarely frequents, and more rarely figures in those convivial societies which are distinguished for the jollity and gaiety of their conversation." Such a social scene "might interrupt the steadiness of his industry, or break in upon the strictness of his frugality." Go to too many parties and you may find yourself leaving work early or spending too much money on your clothes or on the bottle of wine you take to your host.

The prudent man strives to be inoffensive. He is never rude. He sacrifices ease and enjoyment today for greater ease and enjoyment tomorrow. He sacrifices what he wants now for what he wants most. He keeps to his own business and doesn't enjoy meddling in the affairs of others. He gets no pleasure from running other people's lives or taking credit for doing so. When called, he serves his country. But he will not scheme to get into public life. He is happy to leave governing to others. "In the bottom of his heart he would prefer the undisturbed enjoyment of secure tranquillity, not only to all the vain splendour of successful ambition, but to the real and solid glory of performing the greatest and most magnanimous actions."

Having said that about politics and the public sphere, Smith later admits that there is "wise and judicious conduct" that goes beyond the individual. Prudent generals, legislators, and statesman have the potential to combine the steady reliability of prudence with "many greater and more splendid virtues," such as bravery or benevolence, or a regard for justice. Then "it necessarily supposes the utmost perfection of all the intellectual and of all the moral virtues. It is the best head joined to the best heart. It is the most perfect wisdom combined with the most perfect virtue."

Of all the attributes of prudence that Smith discusses, my favorite is how the prudent man treats his intellectual gifts.

> The prudent man always studies seriously and earnestly to understand whatever he professes to understand, and not merely to persuade other people that he understands it; and though his talents may not always be very brilliant, they are always perfectly genuine.

The prudent man is genuine. He is modest about his skills and successes. A simpler way to capture Smith's advice is "Say little, do much."

> He neither endeavours to impose upon you by the cunning devices of an artful impostor, nor by the arrogant

airs of an assuming pedant, nor by the confident asser-
tions of a superficial and imprudent pretender. He is not
ostentatious even of the abilities which he really possesses. His conversation is simple and modest, and he is
averse to all the quackish arts by which other people so
frequently thrust themselves into public notice and reputation.

I don't know what the quackish arts of self-promotion
were in Smith's time. Today, we use Twitter and Facebook
and blogging and various public relations stunts to gain attention for our products, our ideas, and ourselves. Are these
quackish arts lacking in virtue for their imprudence? Certainly relentless self-promotion can feel demeaning. And
the narcissism of our day likely surpasses the worst excesses
of Smith's. That leaves the modern man and woman with a
challenge. How do you maintain your dignity in an increas-
ingly undignified world?

According to Google, there are about 130 million books
out in the world. If I want people to read mine, someone has
to bang a drum, wave a flag, or do some kind of electronic
tap dance to get my book noticed. You have to tweet and
blog and hype the virtues of what you're selling, whether it's
the latest brand of flavored water or something purported

to be closer to wisdom. What's a person to do? Your best bet is to use the modern arts of social media and self-promotion, but as unquackishly as possible.

Most people find self-promotion a little degrading. Or at least they think they're supposed to, so when they mention their own book on their blog, they'll call it "shameless self-promotion" as a way of showing that they realize that what they're doing is a bit awkward. When you're saying "Look at me," it's hard to pretend you're saying something different. Maintaining your dignity becomes a matter of style and balance. The question is how to say "Look at me" in the most prudent and dignified way. For starters, don't lie or embellish. Don't exaggerate your achievements or qualifications. Don't give yourself a degree you haven't earned or claim a tour of duty in Vietnam that never happened.

Knowing your audience helps. The Iron Rule of You says that people pay less attention to you than you pay to yourself. You might think that means you have to really bug people to get their attention. That may be true. But most people don't like to be bugged. I once heard a comedian talk about how he dealt with the credit card company that kept sending him last notices and threats of cancellation. He told them: "Listen, credit card company. I can't pay all my bills, so each month I put all my bills in a hat and take a few out and pay them. You keep bugging me and I'm going to stop even putting your bills in the hat." If you bug someone too much via e-mail, they'll take you out of the hat. They'll just shove you in the spam folder and you're done.

People who enjoy being the center of attention and promoting themselves fare best when they recognize that trait and try not to take advantage of every opportunity to promote themselves. Sometimes it's better to stay silent and miss a chance to mention something that might advance a project. In today's world, you can feel like a sucker for lying low and missing an opportunity. But sometimes it's better to feel like a sucker than a shill.

Smith's prudent man seems a little boring. Even Smith admits that acting prudently about your health, fortune, and reputation, while an "amiable quality," receives only a "certain cold esteem" but doesn't seem entitled to any great admiration. Yet Smith's vision of the prudent man has a certain dignity. And I have to think it captures much of what Smith aspired to in his own conduct.

What about the virtue of justice, the second virtue of the three that Smith emphasizes? At the end of *The Theory of Moral Sentiments*, Smith discusses different kinds of justice. But when he uses the term by itself in the first part of the book and celebrates its importance, he means not harming or hurting others—a negative virtue, the virtue of not doing something bad. Hillel said it a few millennia before Smith— don't do unto others what you would not want done to you. Don't steal. Don't murder. Don't lie to get an advantage over someone. Don't cheat at cards. Don't cheat at school. Don't abuse your spouse. Don't hurt someone's feelings.

One way Smith talks about justice is by invoking the impartial spectator's view of our behavior. In a lengthy passage, he gives an eloquent vision of how we are perceived when we act unjustly. He starts by explaining that the only justification that people accept for hurting someone is to avenge or punish harm:

> There can be no proper motive for hurting our neighbour, there can be no incitement to do evil to another, which mankind will go along with, except just indignation for evil which that other has done to us.

Smith continues by saying that an impartial spectator will judge you poorly if you hurt someone merely to benefit yourself:

> To disturb his happiness merely because it stands in the way of our own, to take from him what is of real use to him merely because it may be of equal or of more use to us, or to indulge, in this manner, at the expence of other

people, the natural preference which every man has for his own happiness above that of other people, is what no impartial spectator can go along with.

Then after conceding the Iron Law of You—you care more about yourself than you do about others—Smith gives a beautiful summary of why it's wrong to put yourself before others. He uses the same logic that he uses in the Chinese earthquake example. Even though you care less about others than you do for yourself, to live that way—to hurt others in order to benefit yourself—is not acceptable to the impartial spectator.

> Though it may be true, therefore, that every individual, in his own breast, naturally prefers himself to all mankind, yet he dares not look mankind in the face, and avow that he acts according to this principle. He feels that in this preference they can never go along with him, and that how natural soever it may be to him, it must always appear excessive and extravagant to them.

When he considers the impartial spectator's view, he will "humble the arrogance of his self-love, and bring it down to something which other men can go along with." Smith closes the passage with a magnificent summary of fair play in the game of life:

In the race for wealth, and honours, and preferments, he may run as hard as he can, and strain every nerve and every muscle, in order to outstrip all his competitors. But if he should justle [jostle, bump into], or throw down any of them, the indulgence of the spectators is entirely at an end. It is a violation of fair play, which they cannot admit of. This man is to them, in every respect, as good as he: they do not enter into that self-love by which he prefers himself so much to this other, and cannot go along with the motive from which he hurt him. They readily, therefore, sympathize with the natural resentment of the injured, and the offender becomes the object of their hatred and indignation. He is sensible that he becomes so, and feels that those sentiments are ready to burst out from all sides against him.

Our self-love may encourage us to play dirty in order to finish ahead of someone else. But when we see ourselves through the eyes of the impartial spectator, we know it's wrong.

The rules of justice are relatively black-and-white. If I owe someone ten dollars, justice requires me to pay him back when I agreed to pay him back. There's nothing complicated or unclear about my obligation. Smith admits there can be extenuating circumstances that make the rules of justice more flexible. But he suggests that such an approach to justice is a very slippery slope. He urges us to follow the rules of justice with complete steadfastness; the more we do so, the more commendable and dependable we are.

Once we start to think that the rules of justice can be ignored in special circumstances, we are no longer trustworthy, and we become capable of the greatest villainy. Smith gives two examples—the thief and the adulterer—of how such rationalization can get us in trouble:

> The thief imagines he does no evil, when he steals from the rich . . . what possibly they may never even know has been stolen from them. The adulterer imagines he does no evil, when he corrupts the wife of his friend, provided he covers his intrigue from the suspicion of the husband, and does not disturb the peace of the family. When once we begin to give way to such refinements, there is no enormity so gross of which we may not be capable.

Remember that Smith sees the role of norms and the "general rules" of morality that we learn from the world around us as a way for us to bolster the voice of the impartial spectator when our passions conflict with what we know is right. Smith's emphasis on the importance of not deviating from the rules related to justice—always pay your debts, never steal, never betray your spouse—is a crucial aspect of confronting our self-deception. Once we decide that these rules can be relaxed in special circumstances, we're on the road to finding ways to convince ourselves that what is good for me is good for you, too. Then there will be "no enormity so gross of which we may not be capable." That's not a mild warning; it's a blaring siren.

Smith understands something deep about human nature with this warning. Hard-and-fast rules are easier to keep than rules that are slightly relaxed. The opposite should be true. You'd think abstinence would be much harder to keep than moderation. Yet it is much easier to give up potato chips than to eat just one. Or a few. But shouldn't it be otherwise? Shouldn't it be easier to limit yourself to a few chips than to have none? Yet a few often leads to a few more. And a few more. Smith counsels us to keep the general rules of justice with the "greatest exactness." They are "accurate in the highest degree, and admit of no exceptions or modifications."

The precision of the rules of justice and the ability we have to keep them with the "greatest exactness" gives us a path to follow if we want to achieve justice as Smith describes it. Beneficence, the third of Smith's triumvirate of key virtues, is another matter. What is the virtue of beneficence? Beneficence means doing good. Not doing bad is pretty straightforward. But how do you do good? What are the rules of beneficence? There are no easy, black-and-white rules, alas. The rules of justice are clear. The rules of beneficence are "loose, vague, and indeterminate."

Smith looks at gratitude, a part of beneficence that seems at first to be pretty straightforward. Expressing gratitude would seem to be an easy rule to follow. Many times it is. If someone lends me $1,000, Smith says that my gratitude should obligate me to lend him money when he is in distress. But am I obligated to lend him the same amount? When? Tomorrow? Someday?

And suppose our financial circumstances are very different. What if his loan of $1,000 to me was nothing to him, but, for me, lending him $1,000 would lead to great financial stress? If instead of money, he asks for the loan of something precious or necessary to me that is worth $1,000? Does gratitude require me to say yes? Smith says that if our circumstances are sufficiently different, my willingness to lend or even give you ten times what you lent me may not be sufficient to show 1/100th of the gratitude I owe you. Under the right circumstances, I can be accused of the blackest ingratitude and deserve the accusation.

Gratitude is one of the simpler virtues that make up beneficence. Smith discusses other beneficent virtues, such as friendship, humanity, hospitality, generosity. Relative to gratitude, Smith says the rules for these virtues "are still more vague and indeterminate."

> The general rules of almost all the virtues, the general rules which determine what are the offices of prudence, of charity, of generosity, of gratitude, of friendship, are in many respects loose and inaccurate, admit of many exceptions, and require so many modifications, that it is scarce possible to regulate our conduct entirely by a regard to them.

Consider the virtue of charity that is part of beneficence— the virtue of helping a fellow human being who is suffering or in despair or in poverty. What should you do to help those who are hungry or struggling financially? You're a tourist in a large city and a person approaches you asking for a handout. Should you give him money? How much? Is it wrong to give him money if you think he's going to spend it on drugs or liquor? Or should poor people be entitled to the respect you show to everyone else, judging them capable of making their own decisions, no matter how much you disagree with those choices?

Should you give every person who asks you for money the same amount, or should you try to discover who is in serious straits and who is not? Perhaps you should give nothing to panhandlers—give instead to a charity that distributes money based on the personal circumstances of the recipients. But what about the people who are uncomfortable dealing with forms and officials and who are living on the street? Or maybe you should give neither to a private charity nor to a homeless individual. If you pay taxes, some of your income is already paying for food stamps. Does that fulfill your obligation to help the hungry? And if it does, should you then give money to a scholarship fund for private schools to allow the poorest children to attend, giving them a chance to escape poverty entirely? There are no easy answers to these questions.

Smith compares the rules of justice to the rules of grammar. The rules of grammar are "precise, accurate, and indispensable." The rules of beneficence and many of the other virtues are like the rules governing what makes for great writing, writing that is "sublime and elegant in composition." There are no specific rules on how to write well.

> The rules of justice may be compared to the rules of grammar; the rules of the other virtues, to the rules which critics lay down for the attainment of what is sublime and elegant in composition. The one, are precise, accurate, and indispensable. The other, are loose, vague,

and indeterminate, and present us rather with a general idea of the perfection we ought to aim at, than afford us any certain and infallible directions for acquiring it.

A person can be taught to write grammatically by following a set of rules. A person can be given a set of rules and taught to act justly.

But there are no rules whose observance will infallibly lead us to the attainment of elegance or sublimity in writing; though there are some which may help us, in some measure, to correct and ascertain the vague ideas which we might otherwise have entertained of those perfections. And there are no rules by the knowledge of which we can infallibly be taught to act upon all occasions with prudence, with just magnanimity, or proper beneficence: though there are some which may enable us to correct and ascertain, in several respects, the imperfect ideas which we might otherwise have entertained of those virtues.

Virtuous behavior is like good writing. We know it when we see it, but it is not easily taught or described with any precision. I don't think Smith says it explicitly, but the imprecision of the rules of beneficence is what makes being good so daunting. It's not just that we aren't sure what to do.

It's that without general rules of beneficence we can cleave to with the "greatest exactness," we can so easily justify doing what is best for ourselves and imagine we are helping those around us when the opposite is the case.

When my son needs my help or wants to talk, I sometimes keep an eye on the football game. I can justify my self-serving behavior in so many ways. I work hard for the family; if I don't relax with a football game now and then, I'm going to jeopardize my effectiveness as a worker and even a father. I can convince myself that I deserve not to pay full attention to my kid. Or I might say to myself that I'm a great multitasker. I'm giving 100 percent of my attention to both my kid and the game; I'm hearing every word he says, aren't I? And if I ever feel guilty about the partial attention I'm giving my son, I can tell myself that it's impossible to give him all the attention he wants. So I have to pick and choose. Yes, sometimes I watch the game while he's telling me about his day or his problems, but that's OK; there are other times when I'm there for him, so I still have a pretty good batting average.

When my kids were young, I read a parenting book that encouraged you to always take your child's hand when it's offered. There will come a day when your child will be too old or too self-conscious to hold a parent's hand, and you'll regret the times you failed to enjoy the moment. After reading that, I created a beneficent rule that was a little bit challenging—I always took my daughter's or son's hands when they were offered. Not only did that rule mean holding their hands more often than I otherwise would have, I usually remembered to savor the moment. And I was more likely to reach my hand out for theirs.

It's hardly ever bothersome to hold your child's hand. But there probably were times when I forgot or, out of inconvenience or exhaustion, missed the opportunity. There are much harder acts of beneficence to keep—giving your friends and family their full attention when they need it, for example. Those rules are harder to keep because the sacrifice is greater than holding a hand when you'd rather have your hand swinging free, but they're also harder because there are times when giving your full attention can hurt the person you're trying to help. Your job really is at stake and you need to finish that proposal; your kid is going to have to do the algebra homework on his own. And, after all, isn't it sometimes better for the kid to do his homework without any help? Aren't you teaching him to be self-reliant when he does his homework without your help? Won't he remember the lesson better if he doesn't have a crutch to lean on?

And of course those excuses are sometimes not excuses, they're explanations. That is, they're true. But that's what makes the rules of beneficence so hard. What we can learn from Smith is to be aware of how hard beneficence is without those rules. Better to have a rule like "Always hold your kids' hands when offered" or "Always give your kids your full attention," even if they're not really universal rules and even if you know you can't keep them with the "greatest exactness." Those unrealistic, unkeepable rules remind you to watch out for your self-centeredness and keep in mind what the impartial spectator might think of you if he saw you watching the game or mindlessly surfing the Internet when your kid has hit a total dead end on that algebra problem.

While prudence, justice, and beneficence were key virtues to Smith, he mentions many more along the way. One of them is friendship. Smith's best friend, David Hume, passed away at the end of August 1776. A few months after Hume's death, Smith wrote a letter to William Strahan, the printer/publisher of both Hume's and Smith's works. The letter talks about some of the last conversations Smith had with Hume and how Hume was coping with the approach of death. The ending of that letter captures Smith's ideal of the wise and virtuous man.

Smith writes that while people may disagree or agree with Hume's philosophical views, no one could question Hume's character or conduct:

Thus died our most excellent, and never to be forgotten friend; concerning whose philosophical opinions men will, no doubt, judge variously, every one approving, or condemning them, according as they happen to coincide or disagree with his own; but concerning whose character and conduct there can scarce be a difference of opinion.

Hume was even-tempered, even when he didn't have a lot of money. And when he didn't have a lot of money, when he was in the "lowest state of his fortune," the care he took with his money never stopped him from being charitable and generous with it. His prudence with his money wasn't greed—what Smith calls avarice—but due to Hume's desire not to rely on others for his needs:

His temper, indeed, seemed to be more happily balanced, if I may be allowed such an expression, than that perhaps of any other man I have ever known. Even in the lowest state of his fortune, his great and necessary frugality never hindered him from exercising, upon proper occasions, acts both of charity and generosity. It was a frugality founded, not upon avarice, but upon the love of independency.

Hume's wit and conversational banter were never mean-spirited—without what Smith describes as the "tincture of malignity"—and never hurt other people's feelings:

> The extreme gentleness of his nature never weakened either the firmness of his mind, or the steadiness of his resolutions. His constant pleasantry was the genuine effusion of good-nature and good-humour, tempered with delicacy and modesty, and without even the slightest tincture of malignity, so frequently the disagreeable source of what is called wit in other men. It never was the meaning of his raillery to mortify; and therefore, far from offending, it seldom failed to please and delight, even those who were the objects of it. To his friends, who were frequently the objects of it, there was not perhaps any one of all his great and amiable qualities, which contributed more to endear his conversation.

Smith closes with praise for how the pleasantness of Hume's company combined with his intellectual gifts and focus to make him such an admirable human being. Smith's summing up is about as good a tribute as you would want from a friend:

And that gaiety of temper, so agreeable in society, but which is so often accompanied with frivolous and superficial qualities, was in him certainly attended with the most severe application, the most extensive learning, the greatest depth of thought, and a capacity in every respect the most comprehensive. Upon the whole, I have always considered him, both in his lifetime and since his death, as approaching as nearly to the idea of a perfectly wise and virtuous man, as perhaps the nature of human frailty will permit.

I ever am, dear Sir,
Most affectionately yours,
ADAM SMITH.

To approach "as nearly to the idea of a perfectly wise and virtuous man, as perhaps the nature of human frailty will permit" is a pretty high level of achievement. Many of us may struggle to reach that level, but Smith is saying that heading in that direction is the right path to being loved and the best way to be lovely. However, many of us want to do more than be wise and virtuous. We want to make the world a better place.

Chapter 8

How to Make the World
a Better Place

You're prudent—you take care of yourself and go through life acting with honesty and dignity. You act justly—you do your utmost not to harm others. You're beneficent—you're kind and good to those around you. None of that comes easy. But many of us long to aim even higher. We want to be more than just a good person. We want the reach of our beneficence to extend beyond our circle of friends, families, and colleagues. We want to do more than simply act with virtue toward those we encounter. We want to have an impact on the broader world.

Extending our reach is part of our desire to be loved—if we

can do something great that reverberates beyond ourselves we will be honored and respected by a larger circle. But I think it's more than that. Just as Smith argues that we want to earn love through being lovely, I think our desire to improve the world is a desire we have for even more loveliness. So however self-centered we are—and we are self-centered—we would like to be seen and see ourselves as contributors to the greater good. And I think most of us actually want to make a contribution rather than merely appearing to be contributors. We want to help make the world a better place.

But how should we proceed? I once received an e-mail from a listener to my podcast asking for advice. He said he had become passionate about economic liberty. He was young. His life lay ahead of him. How should he spend his life to help increase freedom? Should he get a PhD in economics? Become a writer? Start a business, make a lot of money, and donate a healthy part of the profits to organizations promoting economic liberty? Or maybe go into politics? The list was long.

I was humbled by the thought that my correspondent thought I might have some ability to help him. And of course the easiest answer I could give him—that there is no answer—is true. There is no best way to increase economic liberty. More broadly, there is no best way to make the world a better place. Many of your choices can make a contribution, but the difference you will make in the world depends a great deal on your unique gifts and passions and opportunities.

You may not have the skills or vision to start, run, and grow a business. You may not have the discipline to get a PhD. Even if you are totally selfless and your only goal is to maximize your impact on the world, it's hard to know the most productive use of your time and effort. And how do you make sure that what you think is productive actually does make the world better? Sometimes, those good intentions pave a road to a very hot place. How do we avoid unintended consequences from our actions that darken our world instead of brightening it? And maybe, just maybe, your best way of making the world a better place is to be a really superlative husband or mom or neighbor.

Or a really good employee or manager or entrepreneur. We sometimes mistakenly see our careers as the "selfish" part of our lives because we earn money or make profit, while our altruistic acts—giving to charity, say, or volunteering at the soup kitchen or giving blood—that's the work we do for others. We think *that's* what we do that makes the world a better place. We forget that being good at our work helps others and makes the world a better place, too.

Being an extraordinary teacher changes the lives of your students. Being a great boss means creating ways for employees to flourish and use their skills. Running a great restaurant gives people a chance to meet their friends for something more than food–for conversation, for friendship and creating memories. And giving people a chance to pay less for shirts or apples or tires because you've figured out a way to reduce inventory costs and sell those items more cheaply lets people satisfy their desires at a lower cost than they otherwise would have to pay. That in turn frees up money to let your customers take a longer vacation or give their kids music lessons or to have better shirts or to replace their tires sooner than they otherwise would. Doing your job with a smile enriches the days of the people around you.

These are not trivial things. That we get paid to do these things is the gravy, not the main course for many of us. But because we get paid and because we are often focused on doing our job, we can forget the impact we have on others while we use the skills we have been given and the ones we have developed through devotion to our craft, whatever that craft is.

Even when we remember the impact our work has on others, many of us still have a desire to do more than that, to do something without a direct benefit to ourselves, something we aren't paid for, something that helps others without compensation. So we coach Little League, we work at the food pantry, we read to children, we give money to the causes we care about. Most of us feel compelled to do something selfless for a cause or an organization that's bigger than ourselves, in situations where the only reward for our time and effort is satisfaction.

In *The Theory of Moral Sentiments*, Adam Smith points the way to something we can all do that makes the world a better place, something we can do every day. It's not easy to see. It isn't dramatic; it's not something you put on your résumé or can brag about. Instead, it works in the background of everything we do, underlying and affecting almost all our interactions with the people around us. To understand Smith's insight about how we can make a contribution to a better world, we have to dig a little deeper into Smith's view of how the world works.

Google was formed as a corporation in 1998. You can look it up. But there's no official date for when it became OK to say "I'll google that later" or "I googled that last night." Usage of "to google" as "to search on the Internet" spread first in English, then around the globe. Who decided it's OK to use the name of a corporation as a verb?

On the other hand, take Enron, a company that was

known, initially, for its elite talent and, shortly thereafter, for its corruption and dishonesty. Yet *enron* did not become a verb or a noun, even in casual conversation. Of course, I'm free to call a corrupt and dishonest person an enron, but you won't have any idea what I'm talking about. It's an interesting idea, using the name of the company as a noun to mean an unethical moron, say. But who decides if it catches on?

We do. We decide that *enron* is not a noun and that *google* is a verb. We decide in the sense that it's up to us. The strangest part of it is that the management and shareholders at Google are against this choice. They want to reserve the letter *g* followed by an *o* and then *ogle* to mean the company headquartered in Mountain View, California. The amazing thing is they can't stop us from deciding. They can protest, complain, work against it. But it's not up to them. It's up to us.

The only problem with saying we decide *google* is a verb is that while it's undeniably true that it is decided by us, it doesn't match any of the other ways we use the verb *decide* in a group setting. Computer users didn't take a vote. We didn't have a public conversation and convince the people who don't like using *google* as a verb—the Google folks in Mountain View and the traditionalists who find the word *google* unappealing—that it's really OK to say "google" instead of "search on the Web." We didn't agree on a compromise by which we'll use *google* but stop using *xerox* (in place of *photocopy*) in order to get the traditionalists on board. The whole thing just happened without anyone coordinating or managing the decision.

Usually when I write "we decide" you know what it means—reaching a decision when more than one person is involved. But when I write "we decided *google* is a verb," it's not the same thing. We don't have a word to describe the process by which *google* became a verb. The English language evolves through an imperfect process of trial and error and word of mouth. Silent letters persist. Highly irregular verbs persist, making it extremely difficult for nonnative speakers to master English. *Flammable* and *inflammable* mean the same thing, while *decisive* and *indecisive* are opposites.

You'd think it would be better to have a committee to actually decide what constitutes good English and what does not. Maybe. But a committee would have its own problems and imperfections. Who would be on the committee? How would they decide? How could they possibly keep up with the creation of new words? How would the committee spread the word about their decisions? And perhaps most interesting, why would anyone listen to them?

The French actually have a committee to decide what is

"good" French–the Académie française, which consists of forty members. Dozens and dozens of languages (though not English) have such governing bodies. You'd think an organization of forty experts called *les immortels* (yes, it means what it sounds like) could decide what is good French and what is not. But they cannot. People from France often call Saturday and Sunday *le weekend*. The immortals of the Académie française disapprove of that imported American word, but they have not managed to get French folk to use the officially approved *fin de semaine* with any regularity.

There is no committee for the English language. No one is in charge. But English does not evolve randomly. Useful words and useful grammar persist, mostly. Less useful words become neglected or ignored. *Ruthless* survives, but *ruth* disappears.

Ugly words struggle to survive in competition with more beautiful words. What is an ugly word? *Meatspace* is a word that describes the world we live in, the world of flesh and blood. It is the opposite of cyberspace, the virtual world. But I've never met anyone outside the tech world who has even heard of meatspace. I know no one who uses it regularly. It's an ugly word. I don't think it's going to stick around.

And because no one is in charge of the English language, and because the process of evolution is organic rather than observable and mechanical, it is very difficult, if not impossible, to control it. If you purposely want to change something in English, it isn't clear how to do it or whether you will be successful. You might be, or you might not be.

We are left with a paradoxical conclusion. No one is in charge of English, yet somehow we are all in charge. We decide what is good English and what is not good English, but the mechanism by which we decide is unmanaged, unpredictable, and a bit opaque. At the same time, it's not random. English has an orderliness, too, that, while not perfect, makes some sense. It has a consistent grammar that lets us communicate and an incredibly rich palette of words for expression.

There are myriad things in our lives that have this property—the property that they are orderly and somewhat predictable. I have a photograph from the 1920s on my office wall that commemorates the visit of a group of economists to President Calvin Coolidge: a few hundred grim-faced economists standing in front of the White House. Two things are likely to strike a modern viewer: there aren't many women in the picture, and every man in the picture is wearing a hat. It would have been unimaginable in those times to call upon the president of the United States without a hat. A hat was part of the uniform of respect, along with a suit and a tie.

Look at old photos of fans in the stands at the World Series in the 1920s, say, or even much later. Almost all the men are wearing suits, ties, and hats. Not baseball caps, but hats such as fedoras and other styles with brims all the way around. They are dressed the way they would dress if they were going to church or the opera. Or the White House.

Somewhere between then and now, it became socially acceptable for a man to visit the president bareheaded and to attend a World Series game bareheaded and without a tie. It is as if a memo went out in the early part of the twentieth century saying "Hat required," and sometime in the second half of the twentieth century, another memo went out saying "Disregard earlier memo." Who wrote those memos? Who changed the dress code? Nobody, obviously. No one is in charge of what is fashionable or acceptable or proper dress. Yet, somehow, we all decide. What does that mean exactly? What's the process?

Some people attribute these kinds of changes to fashion leaders—influential celebrities who change our styles. On the hat front, some attribute the death of hat wearing to John F. Kennedy. The claim is that he didn't wear a hat to his inauguration, and as a result, millions of American men breathed a sigh of relief and stopped wearing hats. There is only one problem with this story—it isn't true. Kennedy wore a hat to his inauguration, a silk top hat to go with his morning coat and striped trousers. Not exactly Mr. Informal. It's true that JFK was less formal than previous presidents. I suspect, as do others, that he was responding to a trend as much as he was setting one. Celebrities do influence how we behave and how we dress, but rarely does a single individual do the influencing.

So if it wasn't JFK, who decided that men's dress should be less formal today than fifty or one hundred years ago? Who killed the hat? Who created the trend that made it acceptable for an American president to go bareheaded?

So many aspects of our lives look orderly but are under no one's control. Such phenomena include the reliability (sadly) of rush-hour traffic, the price of oranges, the level of noise in a restaurant, the ability to find sushi in any American city with more than fifty thousand people, and a million other things that are the result of what Adam Ferguson, a Scottish contemporary of Adam Smith's, called the result of human action, but not of human design. These things are created by the actions of many people, but no person plans or intends the outcome.

Smith and Ferguson, along with Smith's good friend David Hume, were deeply interested in these social phenomena. The idea that there are things that are orderly but not planned and that emerge out of complex human interactions came so naturally to Smith that he rarely stopped to discuss these phenomena in a general sense. Smith did write about the invisible hand, of course, but by that phrase he simply meant self-interested actions that turn out to benefit others. Which is too bad, because *invisible hand* is a nice way to describe something that looks designed but that in fact emerges from an unnoticed, unseen, and complex web of innumerable human interactions.

F. A. Hayek is perhaps known best for his intellectual battle with John Maynard Keynes over the business cycle and what causes the economy to sputter. He is less known for his writing on the topic of unplanned order emerging out of complex interactions. Hayek frequently used the phrase "spontaneous order," in which *spontaneous* means unplanned. But spontaneous also has other meanings that are quite different. I prefer the phrase *emergent order* to describe social phenomena that emerge from the complex interactions of individuals and that have an orderliness and logic to them even though they are not designed consciously by any individual.

When we say that instances of emergent order are decided by us, that word, *decided*, is decidedly confusing. All the other uses of that term include some kind of process in which the deciders have some sort of intention when they decide. But when I use the word *google* because it's convenient, I'm not really making any kind of decision about the evolution of the English language. However, I play a small part in how the English language evolves. Very small, but a part, nonetheless.

That leads to a second paradox. The way I use the English language is so trivial in the grand scheme of things as to be essentially irrelevant in determining which words survive and which words die. My individual impact is so small it approaches zero. One person acting alone has no impact. Yet all of us together determine the outcome.

The economist Milton Friedman captured this strange paradox of small effects amounting to something significant when he said about supply and demand that the sum of negligible forces need not be negligible. So while my demand for apples has no impact on the price of apples, our demands all together, along with the decisions of suppliers, are what determine the price of apples. Not the greed of the grocer down the street, not my desire to get a good deal, but all our interactions together. And even though any one apple eater has no measurable or noticeable effect on the price, because she contributes an insignificant portion of the total demand for apples, apple eaters as a group have a very significant effect.

Thinking clearly about the complex interaction of individual actions that lead to unintended patterns of predictable and orderly outcomes is, I believe, the single deepest contribution of economics to understanding how the world works. Ironically, Smith's most eloquent description of this phenomenon is not in *The Wealth of Nations*, his "economics" book, but in *The Theory of Moral Sentiments*, his "philosophy" book. And the example he uses is not a monetary phenomenon but a moral one.

In *The Theory of Moral Sentiments*, Smith describes how individual choices can lead to important social outcomes. He's talking about something more important than the price of apples. He's describing the role each of us plays in creating a moral society. You can even make the bolder claim that he is describing the role that each of us plays in creating our civilization, the society that many of us are fortunate enough to live in, which, despite its immense imperfections, is many steps above savagery.

How nice should I be to my wife? How much time should I spend with my children? How honest should I be on the job? Should I take advantage of a friend? A stranger? Much of the time, we have a pretty good idea what the right answer is to these questions according to those in our circle of friends and acquaintances. We often know what is proper and what is improper. We know what people consider to be the minimum standard and what it takes to go beyond propriety. It is as if there are rules of social interaction that go way beyond what we call etiquette—which fork to use and when a thank-you note via e-mail is acceptable.

Where do these rules come from? Who decides what is proper behavior and what is improper? Who decides when it is OK to act selfishly and when it is monstrous? What determines how we treat each other in the myriad interactions we have each day with those around us?

Adam Smith's answer is that *we* decide what is proper and improper, what is virtuous and what is not. We decide these things—the basis for morality and civilization—in the same way we decide what is acceptable English. All the norms that overlay our daily interactions—the trust, the empathy, the respect, the disdain, the rejection, the kindness, the cruelty—all these patterns of behavior around us come from all our actions together in a similar way that language usage is "decided" by all our individual actions together.

Smith argues that each of us acts in such a way that together we create morality, trust, civilization. None of us intends that outcome. In fact, he argues, it comes about naturally. It's part of who we are. No one plans by his or her actions to improve the world. Yet we do so without having to think about it.

How is that possible? Smith argues that norms and culture are the result of the tiny and infinitely numerous and subtle ways we interact. In the same way that what is considered good English evolves, our cultural landscape is created, without design or oversight, by our individual interactions with each other. But Smith is particularly interested in what determines loveliness—the traits of an honorable person of integrity. Where do these come from? Who decides what is honorable and noble and kind? We do, and we decide these things in the same way we decide what constitutes good English. These outcomes are the result of all our interactions together. They are not controlled, determined, or manipulated by any one person. And few of us realize that we play a role in creating these norms and values.

How can that possibly work? What is the process that allows norms to emerge that we affect through our actions? We want to be loved and lovely. When people approve of what we do, we are pleased. When they don't approve of what we do, we are disappointed. This desire to be loved— our desire to seek approval and avoid disapproval, to seek honor and avoid dishonor—is embedded in us by God or nature, depending on your worldview. Also inside us is the natural inclination to give our approval to honorable behavior and our disapproval to dishonorable behavior.

These urges and inclinations are feedback loops that have the potential to create a civilized society. Good behavior is encouraged by approval. Bad behavior is discouraged by disapproval. Those are the incentives created by those around us—the actual spectators of our actions. Then there is the internal regulator we carry with us, the "man within the breast," our self-awareness of our own loveliness or lack of loveliness. This internal guide—activated by our imagining of an impartial spectator—is an additional thermostat. The pride we feel when we are lovely encourages good behavior, and our shame when we behave badly discourages bad behavior.

> The all-wise Author of Nature has, in this manner, taught man to respect the sentiments and judgments of his brethren; to be more or less pleased when they approve of his conduct, and to be more or less hurt when they disapprove of it. He has made man, if I may say so, the immediate judge of mankind; and has, in this respect, as in many others, created him after his own image, and appointed him his vicegerent upon earth, to superintend

the behaviour of his brethren. They are taught by nature, to acknowledge that power and jurisdiction which has thus been conferred upon him, to be more or less humbled and mortified when they have incurred his censure, and to be more or less elated when they have obtained his applause.

How well does the system work? Very imperfectly. But it sometimes works much better than a system of explicit external punishment by a police force. Ask yourself why you don't break into your neighbor's house when you know your neighbor is away. Why don't you strike someone smaller than you who is in your way or who annoys you? Is it because it is illegal or because it is immoral? How much would the world change if the laws against murder were repealed? Yes, we are all animals with a deep potential for violence inside us. But what subdues that potential? Is it our legal system or our conscience and our desire to be part of civilized society? Is it the police or those around us who would judge us irrevocably were we to harm someone else without justification or simply because it suited us?

For years I lived with four people who were smaller than I am and who often annoyed me and kept me from doing what I wanted to do. They are my children. Corporal punishment remains legal in the United States. My parents spanked me very rarely, but I did get the occasional cuff on the head for misbehavior. I always assumed I'd do the same to my kids, and there were times, more often than I care to admit, when I wanted to strike them. But my wife convinced me otherwise, and to maintain her respect and my self-respect, I have never struck my kids. I'm very glad for that. I'm not alone. Most of my friends don't hit their kids. This quiet revolution in parenting has happened without any legislation.

I have no way of knowing whether it's a good idea or a bad idea to hit your kids. Not everything that is socially acceptable is a good idea; not everything that is frowned on by your peers is a bad idea. And in your social circle, maybe refraining from hitting your kids is considered bad parenting. But Smith's point is that civilization is sustained to a great extent by a decentralized system of feedback similar to how we come to our views on how to treat our children when they misbehave. Social feedback that we give and receive influences how we behave and how others behave in response to our reactions.

In Smith's view, this all comes from God—who Smith calls the Author of Nature. In Smith's view, God has delegated to us the role of judge—in our interactions with our neighbors, we applaud, we scorn, we raise an eyebrow, we mock, we honor, we shake our heads. We want to be around good people and we shun bad ones. Smith calls humanity God's vicegerents—a fancy word that might best be defined as "deputies." God has delegated to all of us the job of keeping each other in line. But Smith's not just talking about murder or theft. He's talking about the much subtler interactions we have with each other that determine the people we want to be around and those we avoid. You don't have to believe it comes from God. You can believe it's merely the result of evolution. Either way, your individual actions play a role in creating civilization.

The virtues of courtesy and kindness and thoughtfulness and compassion and honor and integrity are the virtues we celebrate and applaud. There's no way to legislate these kinds of behavior. They are loose, vague, and indeterminate. They fall under the category of beneficence. No statute could be written to enforce them or to punish their opposites. They are best encouraged—and their opposites discouraged—by human interaction. These are the traits that make life good and easy. A world without them would be much less pleasant.

We never stop to think about how it has come to pass that we live in a world that is fairly decent, a civilized world. Yes, we have a legal system that legislates against the worst crimes, such as theft and murder. But our conscience keeps most of us on the straight and narrow. More important, there are cruel and selfish behaviors we don't indulge because norms and culture vilify those behaviors, without legislation. To commit those acts of cruelty or selfishness is to risk not prison or a fine, but the disapproval of those whose approval we desire—our friends and family, along with our colleagues and acquaintances. And ourselves, ultimately, through our desire to be lovely rather than unlovely. This world of decent behavior doesn't have to be created by someone's intention or exhortation. Creating it comes naturally through the signals of approval and disapproval we send to each other and through the admonitions we give to our children. Sustaining it comes naturally. That's a wondrous thing, but Smith also points the way to how we might maintain civilization and even make it better.

We all have two parts to play in that process. The first is to be lovely even when we can get away with not being lovely. When we act poorly, when we take advantage of someone else, when we are cruel, we make the world a little less civilized. But we also have a part to play in encouraging others to behave well and to discourage others from behaving badly. And that is to honor those who are honorable and to dishonor those who are dishonorable. Our accumulated actions create the standards of loveliness. We create the understandings of the impartial spectator that we each in turn use to moderate our self-centeredness.

This doesn't mean making snap judgments about other people's behavior and then reprimanding or snubbing them, or criticizing our friends and family for every mistake they make. There is often more to the story. We are all human and flawed. But we usually know if those around us are good people or not.

Smith isn't saying we should be intolerant. He's saying our choices matter. We can decide whether to laugh at the rude jokes our friends make at someone's expense or at the expense of a race or religion. We can decide whether to pass on gossip that serves no purpose other than to make us feel superior to someone else. We choose our friends. We choose those we won't befriend.

When we honor bad people or avoid good people, we are playing a role in degrading the world around us. It's a small role, almost negligible. But together, our combined actions are decisive. Each step we take away from loveliness is a step away from civilization. As more and more of us take those steps, our seemingly negligible actions are no longer negligible. Through our actions, we create the norms and rules of what is attractive and what is unattractive.

The philosopher Immanuel Kant was a contemporary of Smith's. His rule for personal morality was the categorical imperative. The categorical imperative says that when you are trying to decide on a course of action or when you face a moral dilemma, you should consider what the impact would be, and not just of your own action, but what the world would be like if everyone behaved that way.

Economists love pointing out that it is irrational to vote. Your vote is meaningful only if there is a tie and your vote breaks the tie. Otherwise your vote makes no difference to the outcome. When I point this out to noneconomists, I usually receive a Kantian response—but what if everyone acted that way and chose not to vote? The reply of the typical economist? Don't worry, no one is going to stay home just because you do; your vote simply doesn't matter. That reply is correct. But it shouldn't determine whether you vote or not.

The act of voting usually fails a cost-benefit analysis based exclusively on affecting the outcome of the election. But the categorical imperative implies it is immoral not to vote, unless you think democracy can survive in a world where only a few people elect public officials. Some of my friends disagree; they argue that the current two-party system is corrupt, and that voting only encourages the scoundrels to believe that people actually like the status quo. That's a legitimate argument (though I'm not sure how you make the world a better place by making an implicit statement that you find your political choices appalling). My point is that the argument that it's OK not to vote simply because your vote is irrelevant is not a moral argument, and it shouldn't be. I want to live in a world where people understand and act as if their small actions have spillover effects on the actions of others. So did Smith.

One important characteristic of civilization is trust. When you can trust the people you deal with—when you don't have to fear that your trust will be exploited for someone else's gain—life is lovelier and economic life is much easier. How does trust get created? By the myriad small interactions we have with each other when we honor our word and pass up the chance for opportunism.

Last summer, my wife and I decided to celebrate our anniversary by renting a cabin for a night on the California coast near Big Sur. But there was a problem. There was no time to get the owner of the cabin a check before we arrived so she would hold the cabin for us. Don't worry about it, she said. I'm out of town that day anyway. I'll leave the door unlocked, and you can leave your payment on the table in the kitchen. Can you pay cash? she asked; my cleaning lady will come in later and collect it.

I agreed, but I was uneasy. There was a lot of trust implied in that proposed transaction. She trusted me to pay. I could have just used the cabin and skipped out. What could she do about it? Sue me? She had my cell phone number but nothing else. Her cleaning lady could pretend the money wasn't there when she showed up. I could pretend to leave the money and, when the owner complained, tell her that the cleaning lady must have taken it. And I was leaving the cabin unlocked. Someone else could wander in and pocket the cash.

We showed up, trusting the door would be unlocked and the cabin would be clean. Everything was fine. It was lovely. We never saw a soul, unless the horse on the property had a spiritual side. When we left the next day I fanned out the appropriate number of $20 bills under a cup on the kitchen table. There were quite a few of them. Then I took a picture with my cell phone. I don't know why. There wasn't really a point to it. Sharing it later would prove nothing; I could have taken a picture with my phone, sent it to the owner, and put the money back in my wallet. But I didn't. The owner got her money, and my wife and I had a wonderful day in the redwoods looking out over the Pacific.

Without trust, my wife and I would have missed one of the nicest days we've spent together in a long time. And the owner would have lost a few hundred dollars. Trust is a fine thing.

Here's what life's like without trust, the flip side of my Big Sur experience. A friend of mine told me of a friend of his who was running a conference in Russia. A week before the conference, he received a phone call from the owner of the hotel in Moscow where the conference would be held. Bad news, he said. He could give him only half the rooms he'd promised. He'd gotten a better offer. When the friend complained and pointed out that they had a contract, the hotel owner said, "Sue me," knowing that a lawsuit was unlikely. This wasn't long after the fall of the Soviet Union. The Russians hadn't experienced much economic freedom or entrepreneurship over the previous eighty years. Was the hotel owner a good entrepreneur or a bad one? He had found a way to make more money. But he certainly wasn't lovely by Smith's standards. Without loveliness, the freedom to buy and sell and choose whom you interact with doesn't work very well. The more you can rely on trust and the less you depend on the legal system, the better the system will work.

How do you create loveliness? In some cultures, it's as if a memo went out saying "There's a sucker born every minute; all you have to do is find such people and exploit them."

In other cultures, a memo seems to have gone out that says, "Be a decent human being. It's OK to make money, but keep your word, and don't exploit people in distress." It's a fabulous advantage to live in a society where people resist the urge to exploit others, keeping their word and honoring commitments and contracts even when that means foregoing a short-run benefit. But it's not easy to create trust. There's no easy path to creating a culture of loveliness. And while I think hotel managers in America typically honor their contracts even when a better deal comes along, I get the feeling that, in the run-up to the financial crisis, some asset managers on Wall Street were different, that traders and execs who sold toxic assets knew they were toxic and bragged to each other about their ability to exploit unsuspecting investors. The same was true of mortgage lenders who made loans to people who often were unable to make their payments.

In these industries, loveliness became a liability. Why? We can all understand the temptation to make money off unsuspecting people. Why did the ability to withstand that temptation get weaker? Why did such a destructive norm emerge? At least two answers come to mind. The first is that the rewards to be had from being unlovely increased. Sure, it's nice to be a nice guy. But when being a nice guy costs you a lot of money or when being not such a nice guy suddenly gets more profitable, it becomes harder to resist temptation. The creation on Wall Street of mortgage-backed securities made it harder to be a good person. People didn't get greedier, but the gains from dishonesty rose, so we got more dishonesty.

The other possibility is that the impression (which turned out to be correct) that the government would be willing to bail out the creditors of large financial institutions made it easier for large financial institutions to borrow money cheaply. Instead of investing their own money, they were investing borrowed money. That borrowed money turned out to be backed by taxpayers, not the lenders. And that made imprudence much less costly than it had been in the past. Once upon a time, the giant Wall Street firms were partnerships investing their own money. Whatever culture they created seems to have died when the firms went public and began investing other people's money—other people who were less prudent with that money because they thought Uncle Sam would make the losses good. A culture of trust is very precious and perhaps somewhat fragile. Destroy that culture and there is no easy way to put it back in place.

I once was in Adorama, a superb camera store in New

York City, selling some used photography equipment. I had packaged everything—the camera, a couple of lenses, the strap, the manual, and so on—roughly the way it had arrived when it was new, in the same boxes and packing. Adorama had given me the best price over the phone. Once I was in the store, the salesperson didn't take advantage of the fact that I was now in the store and that going to a competitor would take time and effort. He honored the price I was quoted over the phone.

The salesperson made sure the camera was in good condition. Then he closed the box and prepared to give me the money. I had a couple of lenses in smaller boxes inside the big box. The salesperson made no effort to see if they were actually in there. Maybe I had just put empty boxes inside the bigger box. But he trusted me. I don't know why. And this took place in New York City of all places, a place that has a reputation for sharp dealing.

"Aren't you going to check to see if the lenses are there?" I asked.

"Naw, I trust you," he said.

"Why?" I asked.

"Because if you left them out, you wouldn't sleep well tonight" was his reply.

He was right, though why he believed that to be true is a

puzzle. Whatever the reason, it is so much easier to live in a world where we can trust without having to spend too much time, money, and energy verifying the trust we place in others.

They say goodness is its own reward. But what Smith is saying is that it's more than that. Being trustworthy and honest and a reliable friend or parent or child doesn't just lead to pleasant interactions with people around you. It doesn't just lead to having a good reputation and being respected. Being trustworthy and honest maintains and helps to extend the culture of decency beyond your own reach. You are part of a system of norms and informal rules that is much bigger than yourself. When you behave with virtue you are helping to sustain that system. Every time someone hears you say "google" when you're talking about searching for something on the Internet, you reinforce and spread the use of the word as something more than a brand name. Every time you reward someone's trust or go the extra mile, you are encouraging others to do the same.

And when you honor honorable behavior by others, you are sending out a reward for being honorable. By refusing to pass on the most delicious gossip, even when it's true, you play a role in breaking an unvirtuous circle. By refusing to laugh at the joke that comes at someone's expense, even when it's oh so clever, you are sparing someone pain and refusing to reward the cruelty of the joke teller. Being good isn't just good for you and those around you. It encourages others to be good.

Sometimes it is tempting to forget the categorical imperative and indulge in behavior that comes at the expense of others. It's easy to rationalize—you're so small, how important can it be to do the right thing at any one time? When the waiter undercharges you, is it really such a big deal if you keep quiet just this once? It isn't. But if you go through life with that attitude you degrade yourself, and you are part of those who are discouraging the norms and culture of loveliness. It's so much nicer to be on the other team.

The other temptation is to be pessimistic about the world. It's easy to convince yourself that it's a lousy place and that a single act of kindness that might be a bit of a nuisance doesn't really accomplish much. How do such small steps make any difference? It's tempting to say to hell with it, give up, and just do what feels good for me and forget everybody else. Sometimes when I'm on the Internet and some troll twists somebody's words and humiliates the writer and revels in it, I am tempted to reply in kind, especially when the troll is attacking me. Really, what difference does it make to avoid that kind of behavior? Why not indulge in it, especially when you can do it anonymously? And what's the point of trying to explain something calmly and civilly? The first answer is that it makes a big difference to the person being rude; being a troll corrodes your soul. But, more than that, Smith is saying that every trollish remark is a step away from loveliness, both for you and for others. If we all keep making small steps like that, we'll all end up very far away from where we'd like to be.

There are many ways to make the world a better place. We tend to think of starting organizations that win the founder a Nobel Peace Prize. Or running for political office. Smith reminds us that our small steps matter, too. Less gaudy actions make a difference by joining with the quiet actions of others to create a culture of trust and kindness and respect.

In *Middlemarch*, George Eliot sums up the life of her character Dorothea, someone who was not famous, whose life was spent in the quiet corners of daily life and not in the halls of power or celebrity. But famous people, says Eliot, are not the only ones who make a difference:

> Her full nature, like that river of which Cyrus broke the strength, spent itself in channels which had no great name on the earth. But the effect of her being on those around her was incalculably diffusive: for the growing

good of the world is partly dependent on unhistoric acts; and that things are not so ill with you and me as they might have been, is half owing to the number who lived faithfully a hidden life, and rest in unvisited tombs.

If you want to make the world a better place, work on being trustworthy, and honor those who are trustworthy. Be a good friend and surround yourself with worthy friends. Don't gossip. Resist the joke that might hurt someone's feelings even when it's clever. And try not to laugh when your friend tells you that clever joke at someone's expense. Being good is not just good for you and those around you, but because it helps others be good as well. Set a good example, and by your loveliness you will not only be loved, but you may influence the world.

I like the Talmud's attitude toward transforming the world: "It is not up to you to finish the work. But you are not free to desist from it." You alone make very little difference. But you make your contribution. That's good for you. And when you join in with others, you make all the difference.

Chapter 9

❦

How Not to Make the World a Better Place

Smith's vision of what sustains civilization is the stream of approval and disapproval we all provide as we respond to the conduct of those around us. That stream of approval and disapproval creates feedback loops to encourage good behavior and discourage bad behavior. Our admiration and disdain—properly deployed—encourage virtue. When we are kind and honorable and trustworthy, when we honor those who are kind and honorable and trustworthy, we help create the characteristics of the impartial specta-tor. We create a tendency toward loveliness.

Each action we take affects those around us. The ripples

continue outward as we influence others and as they in turn influence those in their circles. It's like the girl finding starfish stranded on the beach by the low tide and tossing them back into the ocean. A passerby, seeing the thousands of starfish left stranded, tells the girl that her task is hopeless. How can she possibly make a difference? "Made a difference to that one" is her reply as she tosses another one back into the water. Every good deed we do has an immediate impact, but the ripple effects of the impartial spectator and the norms that are created by both our actions and our approval and disapproval of others create an additional impact on the world around us.

But it's a very imperfect system. The rewards and punishments are psychological. We don't always provide the feedback that sustains the system. We sometimes fall down on the job both because of our actions and because of our unwillingness or inability to judge others. We fool ourselves into thinking we're lovely when we're not.

Can't we do better than this? We human beings are so flawed. We don't know ourselves. We constantly make mistakes. And a lot of what we do knowingly is simply wicked. We're cruel. We exploit the weak. We profit from the ignorant. And we know how to fix all that. We just need to discourage the bad kind of behavior and encourage the good kind. Rather than picking up one starfish at a time, rather than doing a good deed here or there and honoring those around us who are lovely, wouldn't it be better to use a shovel? Or, even better, a backhoe? Why not use the government to make things even better? Rather than settling for small, think big!

Smith was a proponent of free markets and economic freedom generally. But he wasn't an anarchist or a doctrinaire libertarian. He understood that governments play an important role in enabling what modern economists call markets and what Smith considered the human propensity to swap one thing for another; what, in *The Wealth of Nations*, he called "truck, barter, and exchange." Smith was a classical liberal, meaning a liberal in the original use of the word—someone who valued liberty and favored limited government. He saw a central role for government in providing national defense, a system of courts, and basic elements of infrastructure, such as roads and bridges, areas where he thought the private sector would struggle without government help.

In *The Wealth of Nations*, Smith occasionally has good things to say about government intervention outside these areas. But there are some activities of government that Smith opposed with great vehemence. One is what now would be called "industrial policy," the singling out of particular industries for government subsidy or assistance. Smith also warned against the dangers of thinking that government leaders could help people figure out the best uses of their skills or capital. Trying to do so would expose a leader to "innumerable delusions," and such a leader would never have the knowledge or wisdom to steer people or capital in ways that would be for the benefit of society as a whole.

But Smith reserved his greatest disdain for what, in *The Theory of Moral Sentiments*, he called the man of system, the leader with a scheme to remake society according to some master plan or vision. He warned that such people fall in love with their vision of the ideal society and lose the ability to imagine any deviation from that perfection. They are blind to those who are harmed by that vision or harmed by its implementation. In his zeal, the visionary—the man of system—forgets that there are certain natural forces that may work in opposition to his plan, upsetting it, upsetting society, and creating unintended consequences.

The man of system, says Smith, thinks he can move human beings with the same ease as the human hand can move the pieces on a chessboard. The problem is that the man of system ignores the rules of chess. He places the pieces here and there around the board as he sees fit, ignoring their natural motions given by the rules of the game.

> He seems to imagine that he can arrange the different members of a great society with as much ease as the hand arranges the different pieces upon a chess-board. He does not consider that the pieces upon the chessboard have no other principle of motion besides that which the hand impresses upon them; but that, in the great chess-board of human society, every single piece has a principle of motion of its own, altogether different from that which the legislature might chuse to impress upon it. If those two principles coincide and act in the same direction, the game of human society will go on easily and harmoniously, and is very likely to be happy and successful. If they are opposite or different, the game will go on miserably, and the society must be at all times in the highest degree of disorder.

The man of system is an apt name for those remakers of society who often claim to be able to remake man—Pol Pot, Stalin, Mao, dictators who had a dream system they imagined they could impose from the top down. The result was as Smith describes—the highest degree of disorder and disaster. Millions died in each of those societies, from famine and the murder of those who actually or allegedly opposed the perfect vision that the leader planned.

But Smith is saying something more than that totalitarians are wicked. He is also giving a fundamental warning to politicians and those who would support them: when you are trying to legislate behavior in a complex world, you have to remember that people have certain natural desires and dreams. Legislation may not achieve what its proponents intend, and it is likely to lead to unforeseen problems. Human beings like to do what pleases them. It starts young; a small child wants the world his or her way and can't imagine an alternative. Legislation that goes against these natural impulses of human desire—legislation that tries to impose its own will on the movements of the chess pieces other than respect what they do naturally—will struggle to be successful and lead to the "highest degree of disorder."

Many of the world's policy failures fall into this Chessboard Fallacy, the consequences of attempting to improve or manipulate people who don't necessarily want to be improved or manipulated. The political failures of the United States in Iraq are an example of the challenges of trying to impose a vision that isn't shared by all the chess pieces. US military and diplomatic policy is a complex system in which the players have all kinds of motives, selfless and selfish. But, in this case, the players' vision of Iraq as some sort of peaceful democracy was not realistic.

Or consider the war on drugs, the attempt by the US government to reduce the availability and use of recreational drugs. I have met kind, empathetic, earnest people who see recreational drugs as a great scourge. And certainly some drug users destroy themselves and their families through their inability to control their desires.

Yet the war on drugs has failed despite the desires of those kind, empathetic, earnest people and despite the harm that comes to drug users. The war on drugs has failed because too many chess pieces have their own movements; too many people like to use drugs. And too many people see those desires as a potential for profit, which it surely is. It's very hard to stop that natural propensity to truck, barter, and exchange. Transactions will take place between people who want to use drugs and those eager to serve that desire because of the profit that follows. You can try to stop them, but it's like squeezing a balloon over here—it tends to swell back out over there.

The war on drugs has failed utterly at the purported goal of the people who led the moral crusade against drugs; it has not eliminated or come close to eliminating the availability of drugs. But America's drug policy hasn't just failed to stop people from getting their hands on mind-altering substances. The war on drugs has created the highest degree of disorder in those places where drug use and drug sales were prevalent. It has created high profits for those sellers willing to risk arrest and prosecution. And it has created violence and death from that violence as sellers competed to get at those high profits. Dealers aren't the only people who died. Innocents have been caught in the spray of gunfire.

The violence has continued up the supply chain and become a war between the drug cartels of Mexico and Colombia, along with the complications that have arisen when the United States has placed demands on foreign governments. Those demands and the subsequent complications all exist because of the willingness of one nation's citizens to fulfill the desires of the citizens of another nation. And despite all the efforts and the incredible expense, those desires are still being fulfilled—evidently people who want drugs can still find them easily.

That's not the end of the harm from the war on drugs. It has corrupted police departments as some police officers and administrators seem to find it difficult not to share in the profits. But even when the police are able to avoid the temptation of actual corruption, they've been encouraged to be more aggressive in seeking out drugs and drug dealers. Inevitably, mistakes are made, and innocent citizens find SWAT teams at their door.

Despite its failure and the associated disorder, the war on drugs persists for a variety of reasons. The police like it—it allows them to confiscate property and enhance their budgets. The alcohol industry likes it because it raises the prices of recreational drugs, making alcohol a more attractive alternative than it would otherwise be. But a lot of regular, everyday people who simply believe that taking drugs is a bad idea continue to support the policy, and that is part of the reason it persists.

People have trouble with the idea that it's OK for recreational drugs to be legal while still discouraging children and others from using them. They have trouble remembering that there are other ways of changing the world than using legislation. They ignore the possibility that the chess pieces' natural movements might thwart their best intentions.

Adam Smith reminds us that sometimes it is better to use other ways of influencing the great chessboard of society. There have been many people eager to ban smoking in the United States, but those attempts have failed. Despite the legality of smoking, per capita consumption of tobacco in the United States fell by 50 percent in the last half of the twentieth century. That's a massive change. Sure, say the critics, but we could have and should have cut it to zero. But that's a fantasy that ignores the chessboard and the natural movements of the pieces on it. Leaving it legal opened up the field for other ways to deter smoking. Some of those ways were legislative—restaurant smoking bans, for example, and taxation—but most of the change was cultural and emerged from the bottom up. Smoking is no longer cool or hip, as it was in the first half of the twentieth century. The cultural norm that smoking is a dirty and dangerous habit emerged with the accumulation of medical evidence and the individual reactions people had to that evidence.

Wouldn't it have been even better to have made smoking illegal on top of those norms? Maybe. But Smith's point is that the world is a complex place. Forces that are integral to the system interact with legislation in unknown, unpredictable, and complicated ways. Sometimes the best way for policy makers to make the world a better place is to leave it alone.

There's a similar lesson to be learned for parenting. Parents struggle to leave their kids alone. We hover and urge and nudge our kids in directions we think will benefit them later in life. And sometimes we're thinking of ourselves; we try to keep our kids from making mistakes we made even when those mistakes helped us become who we are. Or we push our kids to take paths we regret missing.

Inside all of us are two contradictory urges. Yes, all human beings want to be left alone to do what they want. And yes, every parent sees that that desire starts young. But we also like to tell others what to do. When we try to impose our will on our children, we sometimes forget that first principle. So we push our kid to take piano lessons because we wish we had spent more time learning to play an instrument. Sometimes as a result you get a kid who loves piano. But sometimes you get a kid who doesn't just not love the piano; she hates it and never touches one after leaving the house.

In the fable by Aesop, the sun and the wind argue over who is stronger. They decide to settle their dispute using a man walking below them—which one can get the man to remove his coat? The wind blows hard and then harder. But all the man does is clutch his coat tighter and tighter. Then the sun comes out. And the man, suddenly feeling the warmth from the sun, gladly removes his coat. The wind isn't just ineffective. The wind actually gets the opposite result. Paradoxically, it can be better to leave some things alone rather than to try to steer them.

Pushing our kids (or our fellow citizens) to do something that's thought to be desirable sometimes doesn't merely fail. It sometimes leads us to a worse place than where we started. Those chess pieces don't like being pushed around. Lecture your children relentlessly on the evils of smoking and they may end up smoking just for the thrill of defying you. The world is a complex place. When you strive to impose your will on a piece of the system, not every knob you turn will have the effect that you imagine or desire.

The independence of the chess pieces and their desire to go their own ways, ways that the rest of us often cannot fully understand, also reminds us that not all legislation achieves what its proponents intend or claim to intend. Not all legislation is obeyed. Not all legislation is enforced. The fact that legislation is passed does not mean that the problem it addresses is solved. Sometimes the legislation makes the problem worse or masks side effects that benefit self-interested parties.

Smith's advice about the man of system is directed at those who think they have a vision they should impose on the rest of us. Such leaders and politicians are as prone to self-deception as the rest of us. Even when they start off advocating a position just to get elected, Smith argues, they eventually come to convince themselves that it is true:

> Those leaders themselves, though they originally may have meant nothing but their own aggrandisement, become many of them in time the dupes of their own sophistry, and are as eager for this great reformation as the weakest and foolishest of their followers.

Smith's warning is also directed at us, the citizens who want to make the world around us better. He is warning us that utopians can be dangerous and that the world is a complicated place. Sometimes the small things we do in our everyday lives have a bigger impact than the political movements we join and support.

In the webcomic XKCD, a cartoon shows a man at a computer. Someone outside the frame speaks first:

> "Are you coming to bed?"
> "I can't. This is important."
> "What?"
> "Someone is *wrong* on the Internet."

There is a temptation to think that everything important happens in public. There's a temptation to think we can use politics to make the world a better place by creating and supporting good policies. There's a temptation to think that the fights in the blogosphere and on Twitter and Facebook, where we spar with all those who are wrong on the Internet, are actually important.

Smith is reminding us that politics is not where life happens. Legislation and government actions affect our lives in all kinds of ways, good and bad, but we have much to do outside that world. Do you want to make the world a better place? Talk to your kids. Go on a date with your spouse without checking your e-mail. Read more Adam Smith and Jane Austen and P. G. Wodehouse and less of the *Daily Kos* and the *Drudge Report*. Smile at someone you don't know or even like. Be nice to your parents, because you can never repay what they did for you. None of this necessarily shows up in some measure of gross domestic product. These actions don't help pay the bills. They aren't usually on our to-do list, so we don't get the satisfaction of checking them off. A week can go by and nothing will happen if we don't do them. But I think they are the stuff of the good life.

By reminding us of the perils of the man of system, Smith is reminding us to be wary of hubris. We think we can move those chess pieces where we want. We think we know what's best for them. Smith is saying that even when we're right, even if we think we know what's best for others, sometimes it's best to leave them alone, because our efforts won't just fail or fall short of the idea. Sometimes they'll do more harm than good. Sometimes it's best to walk away from the board and set our sights on smaller, better fields of play than the chessboard of society.

Chapter 10

❦

How to Live in the Modern World

The fire is almost out, mostly embers now. My glass of scotch is empty, though it's been refilled, maybe more than once. What time is it? Hard to say. I know I've been here a while. I've gotten to know my host a little better than I did before. He's charming, in part because of his old-fashioned ways. The accent's a delight. But there's more to it than that, of course. He has thought long and hard about the root of things, and he knows how to say what he has to say in ways that get into your bones. It's a time I won't soon forget.

There's one more question I have for the great man, but I think he's a little tired. I am too. I should leave him alone.

It's late. I put my glass down on the small table next to my chair and thank my host for his time.

That last question? It's the one so many fans and some critics of Smith's have wondered about. How could the man who helped set capitalism on its great journey, the man who understood the power of self-interest, the man who gave laissez-faire its intellectual underpinnings, the man who wrote *An Inquiry into the Nature and Causes of the Wealth of Nations*, a book about wealth and materialism and standard of living, how could that man write a book like *The Theory of Moral Sentiments*? There's almost nothing about altruism or kindness or compassion or serenity or loveliness in *The Wealth of Nations*. How can that be? He wrote *The Theory of Moral Sentiments* before *The Wealth of Nations*. He revised *The Theory of Moral Sentiments* after *The Wealth of Nations* was published. Weren't some of those ideas on his brain when he was writing his other great book?

And there's almost no defense of commercial life in *The Theory of Moral Sentiments*. As we saw earlier, Smith is disdainful of material ambition for its own sake. But despite the potential for material ambition to corrode our souls and damage us, Smith does concede, in *The Theory of Moral Sentiments*, that great benefits for others can result—ambition induces us to strive, to innovate, to improve, to accumulate, to produce. In Smith's view, while we greatly exaggerate the benefits of accumulating wealth for our own happiness, ambition is what created agriculture; it made human beings create cities, and led us to discover the great truths of science and the arts and to "embellish human life."

In Smith's view, the great landowner who surveys the produce of his fields imagines he can consume it all; in Smith's words, "the eye is larger than the belly." So when he expands his holdings and cultivates the ground, he thinks he is doing it to satisfy his great appetite. But, in fact, his desires are really quite limited. And so he ends up sharing his great surplus of production by hiring people to work the land and maintain his great house and tend his gardens and maintain his carriages. The result is a decent life for dozens more along the way.

Here is Smith's summary of what rich men of great ambition actually achieve:

> They are led by an invisible hand to make nearly the same distribution of the necessaries of life, which would have been made, had the earth been divided into equal portions among all its inhabitants, and thus without intending it, without knowing it, advance the interest of the society, and afford means to the multiplication of the species. When Providence divided the earth among a

few lordly masters, it neither forgot nor abandoned those who seemed to have been left out in the partition. These last too enjoy their share of all that it produces. In what constitutes the real happiness of human life, they are in no respect inferior to those who would seem so much above them. In ease of body and peace of mind, all the different ranks of life are nearly upon a level, and the beggar, who suns himself by the side of the highway, possesses that security which kings are fighting for.

This is the only time that Smith uses the metaphor of the invisible hand in *The Theory of Moral Sentiments*. And he uses it only once in *The Wealth of Nations*. In both cases, it means that self-interest can lead to benefits for others— hardly the grander interpretation some place on it today. Looking back on the eighteenth century from the twenty-first, it's hard to accept Smith's view that the beggar sunning himself by the side of the road has a similar quality of life to the wealthy and powerful.

But put that to the side. My point is that the best case Smith can make for material prosperity and commercial life within the pages of *The Theory of Moral Sentiments* is pretty thin. He is saying that we have within us great drive and ambition, which serves us poorly as individuals but ultimately has led us out of caves and into the sunlight of civilization. It's a compliment, I suppose, but it's pretty backhanded.

So what was he thinking? How did Smith come to write two books that seem to be so different? The answer, I think, teaches us something about Smith, but something about ourselves as well. Smith's perspective in each of his two great books teaches us something useful about how to live in the modern world.

Before Einstein discovered relativity, before Rodin sculpted *The Burghers of Calais*, before the Eiffel Tower and the Chrysler Building, before Brutus of Troy founded London, before the first human being realized you could plant a seed and wait for it to grow, before the ambition deep within us caused all these changes in the human condition, we were, it appears, hunters and gatherers in small bands and clans. Subsistence was the most one could hope for, and it was not easy to achieve. Life was fragile; death came early and often.

In such a world, how we interacted with those around us made the difference between life and death. There was no insurance company to insure your spear. There was no government to provide disability payments if you broke your leg chasing dinner. People must have leaned heavily on each other. Trust was essential. Failure to chip in, to help out, to do your share, must have been punished relentlessly and cheaply, through shame and anger the first time, but eventually with expulsion and exile if such behavior continued. Every family, every extended family, and maybe every band and clan shared what they had with each other out of necessity.

Primitive life had very small social circles. You saw the same people every day over and over again. Such repeated interactions made it easy to punish those who acted cruelly or selfishly and reward those who helped out the rest of the clan. But it wasn't some paradise out of Jean-Jacques Rousseau. Scarcity was the nature of physical existence. There often—maybe almost always—wasn't enough to go around. Trading with others, either within the family or with nearby bands or clans, must have begun at some point as a way to increase what was available. That would have expanded the circle of interaction a little wider. But not by much. Ultimately, you had to trust those nearest you and fear those farther away. It had to be that way. The difference between life and death was small. There was little margin for error. You hoarded what you had among those closest to you and made sure that those you did not know could not take it away. Your relationships with those around you were everything. There was hardly anything else that mattered.

Modern life is very different. As Adam Smith pointed out in *The Wealth of Nations*, specialization is both the cause and the effect of prosperity, and it creates the modern economic life that allows us to move beyond subsistence. Small groups of people—no matter how talented, no matter how skilled or strong or smart—cannot be wealthy by modern standards over any sustained period of time.

Imagine that you are going to be marooned on a very large, uninhabited island. The good news is that the island is rich in minerals and natural resources. It has flocks and herds of domesticated animals. Its soil is fertile, its climate temperate and pleasant. There are rivers and streams teeming with fish and natural beauty. More good news: You don't have to go alone. You get to take ninety-nine people with you, and you can choose who they are—people who are good at fishing, and at building and surviving. People who understand electricity and metallurgy and many of the skills our modern lifestyle depends on. They will bring their knowledge ánd insight and wisdom. They can bring their books and notebooks detailing any aspect of modern manufacturing and agriculture.

How long would it take for one hundred incredibly smart, skilled, talented, resourceful people to create prosperity? A decade? A century? A millennium? My imaginary island may prosper eventually, but only if the population grows and markets emerge to organize the skills and knowledge of the people to allow them to work productively. Why is the size of the population so important? Working on my own, I might be able to craft twenty pencils a year. But with cooperation and refinement of the production process, twenty people working for a year can produce thousands and, with the right technology, hundreds of thousands of pencils. That's possible because each person can specialize in a small part of the production process. That specialization unleashes incredible productivity. Individuals can work on a part of the process they're good at; when they specialize, they can get better and better, and technology can be applied to each part of the process, leveraging the physical and mental ability of any one person.

So rather than make my own pencil, I work at something else and use the money I earn to buy pencils. By relying on others for almost everything we enjoy—our food, our clothes, our house, and so on—we can enjoy an amount of stuff that dwarfs what our ancestors could enjoy just a century ago. That increase comes from the productivity and innovation unleashed by specialization and trade across billions of people around the world. Without that specialization and innovation—if we had to depend on, say, just our family and friends, regardless of their talents—we would be close to subsistence, the economic reality for most of human history. The poorest people in the world today still struggle, no matter their talents, because they are connected economically only to those who are nearby.

What we call civilization—the comforts of heat, electricity, transportation, medical care, communication, and everything else—requires us to interact with millions of people on a daily basis whom we can never meet or know. Our modern form of economic activity is very different from that of our ancestors. It requires a very different set of social norms and legal institutions that allows us to transact with each other. As the author Leonard Read pointed out, even an extremely simple product, the pencil, requires the uncoordinated cooperation of millions. The power of cooperation that emerges—without a coordinator or manager, through the human propensity to truck, barter, exchange—is often called "the market," but the textbook version of this idea is sterile and mechanistic. Smith understood it as a rich, organic process.

In *The Theory of Moral Sentiments*, Smith argues that we care more about the people around us than we do about others who are farther away. That's why you can sleep well when millions die in an earthquake on the other side of the world. An earthquake across town is a different matter. One that takes the life of a favorite relative is a different matter still. *The Theory of Moral Sentiments* is overwhelmingly a book about the people closest to us, the ones we can actively sympathize with—our family, our friends, and our immediate neighbors. *The Theory of Moral Sentiments* is a book about our personal space—how others view us and how we interact with them. It's not a book about strangers. It's a book about the people we see frequently, some every day, and how our interactions with those around us shape our inner life and our behavior.

In *The Wealth of Nations*, Smith is writing about how we behave in a world of impersonal exchange, which is inevitably a world of strangers. In Smith's day, you knew your butcher, but you did not know the farmer who raised the cow. You did not know the wagon driver who took the cow to the slaughterhouse. You did not know the steel forger who made the knife that slaughtered the cow. Most of the people responsible for the piece of roast or mutton that arrived on your plate in 1759 were unknown to you and unknowable. Today I know even fewer of the people who create the products I enjoy; the power of specialization has been unleashed to a degree that might surprise even Smith.

In a world of impersonal exchange, in a civilized world of global trading, in a modern economy, exchange is often impersonal except at the very end of the exchange, and in today's world, when I order something over the Internet or buy it at Costco, the checker might be the only person I interact with, and even that face-to-face contact is being eliminated by technology. Other than at a farmers market or a crafts fair, I may see none of the people who are involved in creating what I purchase.

If I cannot see the people I truck, barter, and exchange with, it's hard to care about them. I may care a little; I may pay a premium for a cup of coffee hoping that the people who grew the beans are making a little more money than they otherwise would. But, in general, my interactions are almost, by their very nature, self-interested. It would be unlikely for someone to overpay for a car out of concern for the carmaker or even the salesperson she haggles with face-to-face at a local dealership.

Some view this lack of interpersonal interaction as a great loss. Perhaps it is. But it is the unavoidable price of modernity and wealth. Trading only with people we care about or are able to see and interact with would leave us with a very limited number of people to trade with. And that would mean we would be very poor. The "buy local" movement has been successful with a very limited number of products—food and some handcrafted items. The ability to broaden the scope of the movement is very limited. We tried buying local once; it was called the Middle Ages. Of course, people were poorer then than now for many reasons. But one reason people were poor in the Middle Ages was that when you mostly trade with people who live nearby, you are bound to be very poor. There just isn't enough specialization possible with a limited set of trading partners. Self-sufficiency is the road to poverty.

Writing in *The Wealth of Nations*, Smith was interested in how people behave when they trade at a distance. He wasn't just writing about trade with foreigners, though a good chunk of the book is about what we call international trade. He was writing about all kinds of trade with strangers, both within our borders and outside them. When one is thinking and writing about that world, it is best to assume that people are primarily self-interested. And so *The Wealth of Nations* is a book that deals with our self-interested side.

But our interactions with others go far beyond the commercial and the material. We have various circles of friends and family associated with our work, our hobbies, and all the ways we join with others to create community and recreation, pleasure and meaning in our lives. It is those interactions that Smith studies in *The Theory of Moral Sentiments*. It would be absurd to assume that in all our various interactions—as siblings, parents, cousins, co-workers, congregants, bike club members, gym attendees, and every other role in which we interact face-to-face—we are only self-interested.

Smith didn't see us as saints. He saw us clearly. Yes, even in those roles in which we interact face-to-face with people we care about in varying degrees, we often think about ourselves more than we do of others. We may fool ourselves about the loveliness of our behavior. But we do care about those around us independently of ourselves, sometimes a great deal, and we certainly care, as Smith explains with great precision, about what they think of us.

The Theory of Moral Sentiments simply has a different focus from that of *The Wealth of Nations*. It doesn't represent a different view of human nature or a different theory of how people behave or a more optimistic vision of humanity. It's about a different sphere of human interaction. The author of *The Theory of Moral Sentiments* and *The Wealth of Nations* is the same man with a consistent view of humanity. He is mostly interested in how people actually behave, not how he'd like them to behave. He's interested in understanding human behavior. So in the two books the emphases are different because he is writing about two very different spheres of life.

Smith's choice to devote separate books to separate

spheres is a useful reminder of the challenge we face in the modern world. We grow up protected by our parents. If we are lucky, they are loving guardians. They make sure we are fed and clothed. They keep us from the wind and the rain. They soften the blows of life. They share with us without restraint. If we have siblings, they are often treated alongside us in very similar fashion. Not every parent succeeds in avoiding favorites, but egalitarianism is the ideal. We each get the same-sized piece of cake. We take turns sharing special toys.

There is little commercial life in the family, at least when we are young. The rent is free. The food is free. The clothes are free. Free is the only world we know. All the kids are equal. As George Mason University economist Walter Williams has observed, the family is a socialist paradise.

As we grow up, good parents wean us from dependence, and we stand on our own two feet. We find ourselves in a strange and unfamiliar world. We must fend for ourselves. Risk and uncertainty are suddenly everywhere. We must make our own decisions. We are in competition with those around us for the best jobs, for access to opportunity. Unequal outcomes abound.

You might help a friend move into a new apartment, or cook dinner for her when she is overwhelmed by work or just for the fun of it. Our friends provide some of the comfort and security of family life. But even though we make friends at work, we are encouraged to look there for an edge, for a profit, for a competitive advantage. When we call a supplier or even someone in our own firm on the other side of the country, we are confronted with a stranger who almost certainly is unconcerned with our welfare. Yes, there are cultural norms that restrain selfishness in these settings. Equally important are the restraints of competition—my urge to exploit the customer who is a stranger is constrained by the threat of the customer's heading to a competitor. We soon find that even if we do not care about our customers, if we act as if we do we are more likely to be successful. But our workplaces can never be quite like our homes.

There can be something harsh and cold about the commercial world. Good managers realize this and try to create a team spirit and camaraderie that taps into our longings for a more trusting and warmer environment. But a ropes course at a new-employee orientation doesn't make you part of a family. The bank that wants to be your friend is lying. Inevitably, our commercial dealings in the modern world have a physical and emotional distance to them. The inevitability stems from the nature of the modern economy and the degree of specialization and exchange that sustains our standard of living. Too many people we interact with are so far away that we will never see them. To the extent that we trust them, we do so only because of the incentives of competition, reputation, the desire for repeated dealings, and legal restraints on fraud and theft.

At the same time that we begin adult life—interacting with a landlord, an employer, business competitors—we're often starting a family. Once again, we see a stark contrast between the loving world of a spouse and children, where everything is shared and cooperation is generated by love, and the less friendly world of work, where cooperation is generated by the potential for profit and the fear of loss.

These are two different worlds. Nothing really prepares us for the differences. As F. A. Hayek pointed out in *The Fatal Conceit*, a modern person has to inhabit two worlds at the same time—a world that is intimate and a world that is distant, a world that is held together by love and a world that is held together by prices and monetary incentives. Hayek argued that we have an urge to take the norms and culture of our intimate family life and try to extend them into our less intimate commercial life. By that he didn't mean being nice to the cashier at the grocery (assuming your grocery has a cashier) or kind to your co-workers. He meant that we have an urge to try to make the macroeconomy more like the microcosm of the family, taking the egalitarian norms of the family and extending those norms, via the political system, to society at large.

Hayek thought that extending the norms of the family to society at large would put us on the road to tyranny. I don't know if Smith would have agreed about that threat; socialism, Marxism, and communism hadn't been born in 1759. But Smith felt that we cannot extend the love and concern (both selfless and self-interested) beyond our immediate circle of friends and associates. We can only pretend to do so. Whether that pretense is a noble ideal or a dangerous urge is an unanswerable question.

Where I think Smith would agree with Hayek is in our desire to look up to, adore, and entrust our fate to powerful leaders. Out of the womb and out of the house, we often crave security and a parental figure to trust. The problem is that the Hitlers and the Stalins and Maos are not our parents. They cannot love us like their own children, no matter our eagerness that they take care of us. They mainly exploit our longings, meanwhile taking care of themselves. Smith and Hayek are warning us about the danger inherent in that yearning for a politically powerful figure whom we can trust. That danger doesn't exist just with tyrants—citizens in democracies have similar yearnings.

Unfortunately, Smith's insights in *The Wealth of Nations* are not fully understood. We don't teach our children or even our economics students much about what sustains our modern standard of living. Either because of our past, living among clans and bands, or our childhoods, living in a protected environment, we have a suspicion of dealing with strangers and a hostility to the uncoordinated processes that underlie a modern economy. Hayek was right that we need to inhabit two different worlds at the same time to interact within our families and then move into the commercial sphere and interact with strangers. But it isn't easy.

Smith had no interest in romanticizing commercial life. If anything, in *The Theory of Moral Sentiments*, he deromanticizes the quest for wealth. As you can tell from these pages, I think he was undoubtedly right about the potential for ambition and the quest for material wealth to corrode our souls. But I think Smith inevitably underappreciated the opportunities for specialization to be more than just a way to have a higher standard of living. I say "inevitably" because in Smith's day there were wealthy members of the nobility and wealthy manufacturers. But prosperity was not particularly widespread, and much of it—the noblemen and noblewomen, for example—must have struck Smith as relatively unimpressive other than as a way to provide employment for footmen, ladies' maids, and the rest of a royal retinue. Smith was writing at the earliest of stages of the industrial revolution. He was rightly impressed with the productivity of a pin factory compared with a craftsman making pins. But what would he have thought of a modern pin factory? Or, better still, a modern car factory? He couldn't have imagined what was coming.

Nor could he have foreseen the information revolution and the incredible opportunities it has created and will still create for innovation. There wasn't a glimmer in 1759 of the scope that the economy would allow for innovation and the unleashing of human creativity. The dark side of specialization is being the guy in the pin factory in 1759, who spends his day straightening the wire for the pins, over and over again. The bright side is today's specialist in robotics, who creates a way for the surgeon to remove your prostate. Or the surgeon who does the removing all day long and does it perfectly almost every time.

In short, Smith could not have foreseen the way that economic life has gotten easier for so many people and, perhaps more important, the way the modern economy allows people to find meaning and even exhilaration in their work. That phenomenon—the relative ease of modern life for a few billion lives while billions more are able to escape poverty—

could use some romance. It doesn't have the depth of meaning that our families or our communities provide. But it helps us live longer and allows human creativity to flourish, which is part of a meaningful life. It's a phenomenon in which music of very high quality is with me in my pocket, my genome can be used to make me whole, and I can reach thousands of people via the Internet who share my interests and who can answer my questions. I suspect that if we appreciated the role of specialization and exchange in creating the wonders of modern life, we would be more tolerant of its imperfections and more eager to preserve what gives it its power.

Our economic system has to be an impersonal system if it is to continue to deliver the life-transforming and life-affirming gifts of better health, better music, and opportunities to interact with people all over the world. We may wish it to be otherwise. But in a world of specialization, strangers have to play a big role in our lives. And that's OK. Fortunately, I don't have to love the CEO of the company that makes a heart valve or the car that gets forty miles to the gallon or my iPhone. And those CEOs don't have to love me either. They make my life better and more interesting even though they will never see me or feel for me the way my family does. And that's good. Looking for love? Look locally.

We have precious little of it in our lives anyway. Let's reserve it for those we see every day. Love locally, trade globally.

Adam Smith takes my coat from the rack where he hung it and is pleased to see that it has dried. He helps me into the coat and, being a good host, walks me to the door. In the doorway I thank him one more time. This time it's not just for the scotch or the conversation but for everything—his ideas and inspiration and all the time I've enjoyed in his company via the printed page. I step out into the night. The rain has stopped, but a fine mist fills the air. I shiver with the suddenness of the cold. For a moment, Smith stays at my side. Then we say our good-byes.

Leaving is harder than I thought. I find myself lingering on the curb after the door has closed and after I've heard the bolt set. I imagine the great man laboring up the stairs, carrying a candle to light the way. Sure enough, a light glimmers in an upstairs window. Maybe he is getting ready for bed. Maybe he is reading for a few minutes. Despite the cold and damp, I wait across the street, staring up at his window, thinking of his ideas, his insights, all the ways he's enriched my life, until finally the light goes out and the room is dark. Goodnight, my friend, I murmur. Rest well. Then I turn up my collar and head for home.

ACKNOWLEDGMENTS

Dan Klein of George Mason University ignited my interest in Smith's "other book" through our *EconTalk* interviews and numerous unrecorded conversations. Dan created the program in Smithian Political Economy at George Mason; teaching in that program was a great educational experience, and I'm grateful to my students for all that I learned about Smith in the process. My general knowledge of Smith and his ideas has also benefited from numerous conversations about Smith with Don Boudreaux of George Mason and James Otteson while he was at Yeshiva University.

I am grateful to John Raisian and the Hoover Institution at Stanford University for the incredible support and the intellectual environment at Hoover. This book would never have taken off without that support and my time at Hoover.

The title of this book is an homage to Alain De Botton's marvelous *How Proust Can Change Your Life*.

My agent, Raphael Sagalyn, saw the potential for this book long before I did and helped me craft its structure when it was just a vague idea. He has been a great help throughout the process. My friend Gary Belsky convinced me that I really did want to write a book on *The Theory of Moral Sentiments*. More important, when I was struggling to find my voice, he showed me how I could bring the book to life and make it more than just a summary of Smith. His guidance has been invaluable. Adrian Zackheim and Niki Papadopoulos at Portfolio/Penguin believed in the book from the beginning and encouraged me all along the way.

I wish to thank Jonathan Baron, Pete Boettke, Mendel Bluming, Chaim Charytan, Shmuel Goodman, Lisa Harris, Andy Koshner, Richard Mahoney, Emily Messner, Jim Otteson, Aryeh Roberts, Yael Roberts, Bevis Schock, Patience Schock, Orlee Turitz, Barry Weingast, Jeff Weiss, and Amy Willis for their encouragement, support, and feedback on the manuscript.

I am grateful to Gary Belsky, Dan Klein, Lauren Landsburg, Joe Roberts, Shirley Roberts, and Ted Roberts for incredibly detailed comments on the manuscript. Their diligence and insights improved this book immensely. Patricia Fogarty did an excellent job copyediting the manuscript and discovering passages that needed improvement. All the *whoms* are hers. My editor at Portfolio/Penguin, Niki Papadopoulos, made this book better in so many ways. She helped me see more effective ways to structure each chapter, and her comments throughout the book have improved every page.

As always, my wife, Sharon, was my unofficial editor and official shoulder of comfort through the inevitable ups and downs that come with writing a book. She makes everything worthwhile. I am blessed to go through life with someone who is both loved and ever so lovely.

SOURCES AND ADDITIONAL READING

We are fortunate to live at a time and in a world where billions of people can read *The Theory of Moral Sentiments* in its entirety at no charge. You are likely to be in that lucky group, so get reading. All the quotes I've used in this book are from the sixth edition (1790) of *The Theory of Moral Sentiments* (http://www.econlib.org/library/Smith/smMS.html) at the Library of Economics and Liberty (econlib.org). There you will also find Adam Smith's better-known masterpiece, *An Inquiry into the Nature and Causes of the Wealth of Nations.*

Chapter 1
My six-part interview with Dan Klein on *The Theory of Moral Sentiments* is available at EconTalk.org. Dan organizes his thinking on the book in a way that's very different from mine. Readers who enjoy my book will get a kick out of Dan's perspective and will learn a great deal from it, as I did.

My biographical sketch of Adam Smith is drawn from

John Rae's charming and readable *Life of Adam Smith*, published in 1895 (http://www.econlib.org/library/YPDBooks/Rae/raeLS.html). I also learned from Nicholas Phillipson's *Adam Smith: An Enlightened Life* (Yale University Press, 2012). My interview with Phillipson is available at Econ Talk.org.

The Joseph Schumpeter quote about Adam Smith's relationship with women is from Schumpeter's *History of Economic Analysis* (Oxford University Press, 1996).

Chapter 2

One of the funniest and shortest illustrations of the Iron Law of You can be found in the Stephen Leacock story "My Lost Dollar." A brilliant comic writer, Leacock was also a professor of political economy at McGill University.

You can find Jonathan Haidt's thoughts on whether morality is innate or learned in his fascinating book *The Righteous Mind: Why Good People Are Divided by Politics and Religion* (Pantheon Books, 2012). Haidt does not quote Smith, but he does quote Hume quite a bit, and it's clear from those quotes how much Hume and Smith thought alike about morality and self-deception. But the concept of the impartial spectator is pure Smith.

Chapter 3

The Peter Buffett story is taken from his book, *Life Is What You Make It: Find Your Own Path to Fulfillment* (Three Rivers Press, 2011). When the book was published, had he retained his stock in Berkshire Hathaway, it would have been worth $72 million. I've updated the number to the value in 2014—about $100 million.

Bernard Madoff's reaction at being arrested—reportedly one of relief—is taken from James Stewart's *Tangled Webs: How False Statements Are Undermining America: From Martha Stewart to Bernie Madoff* (Penguin Press, 2011).

Chapter 4

This chapter draws on ideas I first discussed in "Pigs Don't Fly: The Economic Way of Thinking About Politics" at Econ Lib.org. Conversation with Bruce Yandle furthered my understanding of self-deception. Through the magic of YouTube, you can watch Richard and Mimi Fariña sing "Pack Up Your Sorrows," a song that is part of my youth. The story of Richard Fariña's death and the reactions of Mimi and Joan Baez comes from David Hajdu's *Positively 4th Street: The Lives and Times of Joan Baez, Bob Dylan, Mimi Baez Fariña, and Richard Fariña* (Farrar, Straus and Giroux, 2001).

F. A. Hayek's views on the faux scientific nature of macroeconomics can be found in his Nobel Prize address, "The Pretence of Knowledge," at nobelprize.org. Nassim Taleb's insights on self-deception and the limits of reason in an uncertain world have deeply affected my understanding of these issues. See *Fooled by Randomness: The Hidden Role of Chance in Life and in the Markets* (Random House, 2001); *The Black Swan: The Impact of the Highly Improbable* (Random House, 2007); and *Antifragile: Things That Gain from Disorder* (Random House, 2012). I've also learned from Jonathan Haidt's thoughts on self-deception and the limits of reason in *The Righteous Mind*, mentioned in the notes on chapter 2, above. My interviews with Taleb and Haidt on these topics can be found at EconTalk.org.

The struggle of Ignác Semmelweis to convince the world that doctors were spreading puerperal fever is from Sherwin Nuland's *The Doctors' Plague: Germs, Childbed Fever, and the Strange Story of Ignác Semmelweis* (W. W. Norton, 2003).

Chapter 5

The story of the Mexican fisherman and the MBA can be found on the Internet in various incarnations; this is my own take, framed to echo Smith's recounting of Plutarch. A similar theme can be found in Leo Tolstoy's haunting "How Much Land Does a Man Need?"

The story about Ted Williams, Jimmy Carroll, and Williams's car is from Leigh Montville's *Ted Williams: The Biography of an American Hero* (Doubleday, 2004).

John Rae's story about Adam Smith arriving late for the dinner party and Pitt's compliment that all the guests were Smith's students may be apocryphal. Pitt certainly admired Smith.

Chapter 7

The full text of Smith's letter to William Strahan on the death of David Hume can be found in the front matter of Hume's *Essays, Moral, Political, and Literary,* edited by Eugene F. Miller (http://www.econlib.org/library/LFBooks/Hume/hmMPL0.html).

The phrase "Say little, do much" is found in the Talmud in Avot, chapter 1, verse 14.

Chapter 8

My novel *The Price of Everything: A Parable of Possibility and Prosperity* (Princeton University Press, 2008) explores the idea of emergent order, the central concept of this chapter. For Hayek's insights, start with "The Use of Knowledge in Society," published from the *American Economic Review* (1945) available at EconLib.org. Then try *The Fatal Conceit: The Errors of Socialism* (University of Chicago Press, 1990).

The insight from Milton Friedman that the sum of negligible effects need not be negligible is found in his book *Price Theory* (Aldine Transaction, 1976).

Did *The Theory of Moral Sentiments* influence Immanuel Kant? Samuel Fleischacker's exploration of this question can be found in "Philosophy in Moral Practice: Kant and Adam Smith," in *Kant-Studien* 82 (3): 249–69 (1991).

My essay on the financial crisis, "Gambling with Other People's Money: How Perverted Incentives Caused the Financial Crisis," looks at the causes and effects of Wall Street's use of debt. It can be found at mercatus.org.

On the importance of trust, see David Rose's *The Moral Foundation of Economic Behavior* (Oxford University Press, 2011), and my *EconTalk* interview with him.

The quote from the Talmud that concludes this chapter is taken from Avot, chapter 2, verse 19.

Chapter 10

Leonard Read's marvelous essay on emergent order and unplanned cooperation, "I, Pencil," can be found at EconLib.org.

Much of this chapter is my take on the so-called Adam Smith problem—how did the man who wrote *The Theory of Moral Sentiments*, which focuses on sympathy and altruism, also write *The Wealth of Nations*, a book that assumes we are all self-interested? And how did he write each book with so little reference to the motivations examined in the other?

James Otteson's answer is found in our *EconTalk* conversation and in his book *Adam Smith's Marketplace of Life* (Cambridge University Press, 2002). For Otteson, both of Smith's books are looking at emergent order—in one case, the emergence of the norms of social interaction, and in the other, the emergence of prices and other economic variables. Jonathan Wight's *Saving Adam Smith: A Tale of Wealth, Transformation, and Virtue* (Financial Times/Prentice Hall, 2001) argues for the importance of both books in appreciating Smith's view of capitalism. Samuel Fleischacker's *On Adam Smith's "Wealth of Nations": A Philosophical Companion* (Princeton University Press, 2004) looks at the philosophical influences of *The Theory of Moral Sentiments* on *The Wealth of Nations*.

Ronald Coase in his essay "Adam Smith's View of Man," found in *Essays on Economics and Economists* (University of Chicago Press, 1994), comes to a similar conclusion to mine on the Adam Smith problem, though he pushes the importance of self-love in both books more than I do here. He also is more focused on the implications for government intervention. His essay is worth reading if only for its superb, brief overview of Smith's view of human nature in *The*

Theory of Moral Sentiments. I thank Dan Klein for bringing Coase's essay to my attention when this book was mostly finished, though I wonder if I had read it before and been influenced without realizing it.

For more on how population drives specialization and prosperity, see my *EconTalk* episode on Smith, Ricardo, and trade.

In this chapter, I quote the passage from *The Theory of Moral Sentiments* in which Smith seems to equate the happiness of a beggar sunning himself by the side of the road with that of a king:

> In ease of body and peace of mind, all the different ranks of life are nearly upon a level, and the beggar, who suns himself by the side of the highway, possesses that security which kings are fighting for.

I suggested that this seems a bit extreme. Is a sunbathing beggar really as secure as a king? Thomas Martin, in "The Sunbathing Beggar and Fighting Kings: Diogenes the Cynic and Alexander the Great in Adam Smith's 'Theory of Moral Sentiments'" (*Adam Smith Review*, volume 8), has suggested that Smith is actually writing about one particular sunbathing beggar–Diogenes–who, when Alexander the Great asked what he could do for him, replied that he could move because he was blocking the sun. Diogenes's contentment was not typical of all beggars. In Martin's view, Smith wasn't arguing that wealth was irrelevant for security. He was arguing that one's philosophical perspective can be sufficient for achieving security. I thank Dan Klein for this reference.

INDEX

He just wanted a decent book to read ...

Not too much to ask, is it? It was in 1935 when Allen Lane, Managing Director of Bodley Head Publishers, stood on a platform at Exeter railway station looking for something good to read on his journey back to London. His choice was limited to popular magazines and poor-quality paperbacks – the same choice faced every day by the vast majority of readers, few of whom could afford hardbacks. Lane's disappointment and subsequent anger at the range of books generally available led him to found a company – and change the world.

'We believed in the existence in this country of a vast reading public for intelligent books at a low price, and staked everything on it'
Sir Allen Lane, 1902–1970, founder of Penguin Books

The quality paperback had arrived – and not just in bookshops. Lane was adamant that his Penguins should appear in chain stores and tobacconists, and should cost no more than a packet of cigarettes.

Reading habits (and cigarette prices) have changed since 1935, but Penguin still believes in publishing the best books for everybody to enjoy. We still believe that good design costs no more than bad design, and we still believe that quality books published passionately and responsibly make the world a better place.

So wherever you see the little bird – whether it's on a piece of prize-winning literary fiction or a celebrity autobiography, political tour de force or historical masterpiece, a serial-killer thriller, reference book, world classic or a piece of pure escapism – you can bet that it represents the very best that the genre has to offer.

Whatever you like to read – trust Penguin.